Keep Calm

The New Mum's Manual

Trust Yourself and Enjoy Your Baby

Dr Ellie Cannon

Vermilion
LONDON

1 3 5 7 9 10 8 6 4 2

First published in 2014 by Vermilion, an imprint of Ebury Publishing
A Random House Group company

The Random House Group Limited Reg. No. 954009

Addresses for companies within the Random House Group can be
found at www.randomhouse.co.uk

The Random House Group Limited supports the Forest Stewardship
Council® (FSC®), the leading international forest-certification
organisation. Our books carrying the FSC label are printed on FSC®-
certified paper. FSC is the only forest-certification scheme supported by
the leading environmental organisations, including Greenpeace.
Our paper procurement policy can be found at
www.randomhouse.co.uk/environment

Printed in the UK by CPI Group (UK) Ltd, Croydon, CR0 4YY

ISBN 9780091954888

To buy books by your favourite authors and register for offers visit
www.randomhouse.co.uk

For my own babies,
Lottie and Jude

Contents

Foreword

Wow, Dr Ellie's amazing book really is a must-read for all first-time mums and dads – and for that matter second-, third- and fourth-time mums like myself.

I hold my hands up and admit that, yes, I am a neurotic parent. I scrutinise and stress over every little part of motherhood – and, believe me, that covers a lot of uncharted territory! I have spent endless hours poring over my laptop in a panic, googling all sorts of medical worries and questions (as you might imagine, 'leaky boobs' doesn't always give you quite the desired results!) Dr Ellie eliminates all this confusion with her book, covering everything you need to know from routines and sleeping to exercising and poo – and that's just the parents!

She gives you the confidence to be a mum and to follow that all-important maternal instinct that will calm your wildest fears and help you make sense of what is a bewildering – yet the most incredible – experience of your life.

A vital read for any parent who feels jaded and confused by parenthood, *Keep Calm: The New Mum's Manual* gives you the absolute confidence to soldier on and feel reassured that you are making all the right decisions for you and your baby. Buddy was my fourth baby, but I still frantically rang my doctor on a regular basis to ask why he slept so much. I believed it wasn't normal and was sure he had some terrible illness. Of course, Buds was perfectly healthy – I only had to glance over at my husband snoozing away on the sofa to realise that actually that's what boys do!

If only I had read *Keep Calm: The New Mum's Manual* I would have saved myself a lot of worry (and a fortune in phone bills!). Dr Ellie is like the angel on your shoulder. She guides you gently through the ups and downs of parenthood and silences that nagging voice inside your head – you know, the one that makes you doubt yourself; the one that makes you feel guilty that you should be doing more. I guarantee that by reading this book you'll worry less, stop comparing yourself to other mums and be confident that you're doing a great job. Most importantly, you'll enjoy being a mummy that much more. This may well be *the* book that stops me wishing I had married a doctor and not my gorgeous chef husband!

Jools Oliver

Introduction

This book is not about babies. It is about YOU – how you can learn to be a confident, happy mummy. That is my only aim. From my experience as a doctor and a mum, I know you don't need a bible to dictate how to look after your baby: you need a best friend to spur you on, encourage your own instinct and point out the two or three rules that are important. That's what this book is about – teaching you faith in your own capability as a super-mamma and giving you permission to relax and focus on the good stuff. Because there's a lot of good stuff!

I have looked after hundreds of new mummies and their babies. I have had two babies myself. I have mothered, supported, listened, laughed, cried, screamed and learnt. The most important thing that I have learnt is that there are a thousand rules on parenting, and most of them are utter drivel.

Parenting is not a precise science, it is a wishy-washy art form and there aren't always exact outcomes and answers behind everything. Babies don't always follow the plan of what they're *supposed* to be doing: they don't follow the rules. That is why I am so anti-rules for mummies. I notice in clinic we try to look for exact non-existent answers too often. Perhaps it is because of the proliferation of science and medical knowledge we expect an answer to everything. Well, I'm sorry but there isn't an answer to everything in the baby-world.

This is not Dr Ellie's guide to creating a genius quinoa-eating baby. This is me telling you, you actually know what to do already. The whole ethos of my Keep Calm approach is to help you find your own way and trust your instinct. You can form your own opinion on the rules, guidelines and mantras that will bombard you.

This is true for all new parents. Most of my experience of working with new parents has really been all about mums: it's mums who turn up to my clinic mostly (not always) and they inspired me to write this book. So for the purposes of the book my advice is directed towards mums rather than dads: but of course it extends to dads too, who also need to learn to trust their instinct.

Me and my babies

I've looked after hundreds of mummies in my GP surgery. I look after them when they're pregnant and I watch their kids grow up through winters of snot and summers of broken arms.

And what I see time and time again is mums who are fabulous but don't trust themselves. And don't enjoy their babies enough. They spend far too much time worrying about minutiae they've been bombarded with. So I wanted to shout out to all new mummies and say ENJOY PARENTHOOD!

It is very hard to build confidence as a parent, especially in the early days, and it's because that's exactly how I felt as a new mum that I want to empower new mums to take back that power so that they can spend days smiling, not feeling guilty for no reason.

I can honestly say I had absolutely no idea what I was doing when I first became a mother. I was 26, already married and working in a hospital. I had a house, worked full time and dealt with life-and-death situations day to day, not to mention a husband. I carried on working night shifts right through my pregnancy; on my last day before maternity leave, I thought nothing of teaching my junior how to do a complicated procedure despite the humongous bump in between the patient and me. I was uber-confident. I read books on parenting, went to the antenatal classes and generally felt like a super-woman! (I never did any cooking but don't let that cloud this rosy picture I'm painting.) The point is I felt ready to be a parent and felt confident in my ability as a mum, even though I hadn't given birth yet. My baby girl even arrived on her due-date – what an achiever already!

Shockingly for me when she did arrive, I lost all that self-belief. I felt confused, exhausted and really lost a lot of confidence in what I was doing. I didn't trust myself enough and sought advice from anywhere and everywhere. Parenthood didn't really feel like it was going 'right' from the things I'd read. My baby didn't seem to follow the routines the book had suggested. Feeding hadn't started the way the guidelines promised. I also spent far too much time worrying about what my friends' babies were doing to notice mine was doing just fine. I spent a lot of time feeling anxious about what tomorrow would bring rather than enjoying today. I had been the calmest most professional woman and I was turned into a neurotic madwoman.

And actually my daughter was a 'good' baby. She was pretty easy and completely healthy, but I stressed about the silliest of things – that half ounce of milk left in the bottle, what eternal damage I'd done by giving her pear not apple as her first fruit; one health visitor told me she was fat, another told me she was perfect. I was confused and bewildered! What I really needed was someone to get a megaphone and shout in my ear – TRUST YOURSELF and CALM DOWN.

When I started in general practice, I could see that a huge number of mummies felt the same way. So I made it my mission to tell you mums to trust yourselves, keep calm and not to lose your own confidence, which is more useful than the advice of a thousand baby experts.

Once second children come along, parents are chilled and they're calm – even I was. And, believe me, that's not simply because they know one end of a nappy from another. It's far deeper than that. It's because they trust themselves to know what they're doing and they have the confidence from experience. They know what to worry about and they ignore the rest of the mummy-mantras and parenting-piffle.

I want to give you as a new mum that confidence in your ability even from day one. You don't need to have had a tribe of children to know what you're doing. You have to have faith in yourself from the start. You have the instinct and all the capability anyone needs to look after a baby, and you must trust yourself to do a fantastic job. Because I promise you, you will.

- Keep calm
- Trust your instinct
- Listen to the baby expert: YOU

Chapter 1

Hello Brand New Mummy – Confidence from Day One

You'll be reassured to know that babies are not complicated. Parenting may now be a multi-billion pound industry, but the fact of the matter is you need very little to be a good parent. And what you do need is already inside you. Being a good mum is not about having the right steriliser – it's about loving your baby (you're already doing that) and trusting yourself (you'll learn to do that). You don't need an encyclopaedic manual telling you how to look after your baby. In the same way you don't need a guide on how to fall in love – it just happens. A spark flies, it's instinctive, it's natural and that's what you as a parent will do. It's a human impulse. Nothing more, nothing less. Just love.

Mummies do need some guidance and help. You need support and encouragement and confidence. But as I have seen and experienced myself, there seem to be far too many people dictating what parents should do. When you first become pregnant a million rules about parenting become apparent, everywhere you turn. I want to show you there are very few you need to worry about, and the rest can be filed under H for hogwash.

If you let yourself, you will be told how to cuddle your baby, what bib he should have and even when you're allowed to go back to work. There is far too much dogma concerning babies and it can drive new parents absolutely bananas. But weirdly, despite the vast swathes of advice, no one seems to learn the important stuff: so I see mummies coming to me from antenatal classes well versed in placental delivery (not important), yet they don't know how to tell if baby is dehydrated (very important).

Guidelines *can* be vital, of course they can: telling parents to put babies to sleep on their backs has saved countless lives from cot death. But for every sensible guideline that's out there, there are a thousand others that you can ignore. This book redresses the balance between the important guidelines and the unnecessary ones.

You are the expert

The vast array of unimportant guidelines that new mums face unfortunately undermines their almighty MUMMY-POWER. That matriarchal confidence our grannies and great grannies had buckets of, gets watered down if we're told what to do at every juncture. Mums do know best: it's a cliché because it's true, and from day one you mustn't let your fabulous instinct be diluted by pseudo-experts.

As far as your baby is concerned, you are the genuine expert. You are a superior uber-mother, and your baby needs you to be happy and believe in yourself.

I can't give you a regime that will guarantee your baby will love mackerel and sweet potato; I am not offering a money-back guarantee that your baby can sleep through the night aged three-and-half weeks. I won't promise you won't have times where you feel tired, fed up and quite frankly a bit lost. But I will assure you that if you trust yourself and believe in your ability as a mother, you will do it right and you will find motherhood as happy and fulfilling as it should be.

Of course there will be times when your hair is high-lighted with breast milk, your hands are covered in poo and your house looks like the back end of a failing laundry. You will think to yourself, 'Am I enjoying this madness?' Quite frankly, no you won't be. Of course you will have moments when you hark back to the days of free-flowing mojitos and Sunday morning sex, and wonder if you will ever fit into those jeans again. This is utterly normal and no encyclopaedia on parenting is going to prevent that. But those moments will be a drop in the ocean compared to the happiness and enjoyment mummy-hood should be. So you mustn't allow anything nor anyone to stop you enjoying and revelling in being a mummy. You need confidence as a mother and self-esteem and support. You don't need unnecessary rules, interference or any well-meaning experts.

No one can teach you how to be a good mother. Nobody out there has the magic formula to 'successful' parenting. A loving mother is a successful mother as far as I am concerned, and so you are already there. Babies need oodles (that is a scientific unit incidentally) of love and that's really it.

You're doing it right

There are a million ways to bring up a baby and yours will be right. Every baby is different and every mum will be. Whether you're the type to crochet your own baby clothes, or whether you think your baby needs to fit into your high-octane lifestyle, it doesn't really matter. If it feels right to you – it is right. If you feel content and positive about your choices, then you are already a great mother. Don't allow yourself to be steered into thinking you're doing it wrong by often well-meaning folk who undermine that mummy super-power you already have.

No one can say only their parenting way is right. I see so many different mummies and many of them have polar opposite views of how to raise a baby. Routine or no routine, breast or bottle. They're all doing it differently, but they're all doing it right.

Mummies need a bit of guidance. A soupçon of advice. What you don't need is an ambush of dogma and opinion that only serves to confuse and destabilise you as the all-knowing professional on your baby.

- Trust yourself, you are super-mum and baby-expert extraordinaire

- You are now a leader in the field of parenting
- Keep calm and listen to your instinct

Trust your maternal instinct

I don't believe in ghosts, Santa, the tooth fairy or cellulite cream. I don't trust magicians, payday loans or stick-thin women who claim they eat chips. I'm highly sceptical about any form of heaven, UFOs, Reiki and all cold-callers. But I do believe in maternal instinct.

I am a Cambridge-educated doctor who trusts science and evidence. I have an incredibly conventional approach to medicine and healthcare and disease. In my work we make decisions based on trials and tangible data. I don't prescribe drugs that 'might' work; I give drugs that are proven to work. BUT I believe 100 per cent in maternal instinct. We can't see it, scientists can't quantify it and nobody can explain it. There is no scientific data to back it up, but maternal instinct is all-powerful and present deep down inside every mummy, from the moment those pesky contractions start. Probably even a bit before.

You have the instinct to bring up your baby – all you need to do is learn how to trust it. It can get a little frayed by well-meaning meddlers, and the barrage of advice. But it is there and you must have faith in your own intuition as a mum.

Instinctively you will know when things are going right, and you will know when things are going wrong. Ask your-self, if you were isolated for a few days with your baby with no WiFi, no healthcare professionals and no encyclopaedia, would you know what to do? Of course you would.

For thousands of years mums have relied on their instinct to know best, and for thousands of years it has worked. For millions of mums around the world today it is working as they bring up their babies in the absence of the internet, manuals and pseudo-experts.

I didn't learn the value of maternal instinct from being a mother. I learnt it long before when I was a medical student. When I was training in paediatrics I had a rather ancient paediatrics professor: the kind of guy who wouldn't have looked out of place in a Harry Potter film, without the wand of course. Over decades of a career he had published case studies, written books and was highly regarded in his field. He was incredibly no-nonsense: someone I learnt a great deal from. One of the first questions he asked my classmates and me when we started was:

'What is usually the first sign that a child is unwell?'

'A high temperature?' someone replied.

'No.'

'A rash?'

'No.'

'Loss of appetite.'

'No.'

Nobody knew the answer, not even the real clever-clogs in the group.

The professor then said, 'The first sign that a child is not well is that their mother is worried about them. If a mother ever comes in and tells you her baby is not right, you listen, whatever the circumstances.' And that is an adage I have always followed and it has always been proven to be right. Mothers instinctively know if their baby is unwell, not from an obvious clinical sign: just because they know. There is not a tangible reason. Perhaps something in the way they look, they smell, their behaviour. Mothers just know. Doctors trust your instinct to be right, so you should too.

Instinct is not only about knowing when things are wrong, it's about knowing when things are right. If your instinct tells you everything is okay, then it is despite what is going on around you. So if it seems okay to you that baby is having carrot with every meal, it doesn't really matter that baby next door is already eating eight varieties of root vegetable.

- Don't let your instinct be drowned out
- Trusting and using your instinct will help it grow, and take control
- Your instinct is worth a thousand baby experts

Feeling guilty is not on the agenda

What I have seen mums feel guilty about	What mums should feel guilty about
Having pain relief during labour	
Breastfeeding	
Bottle-feeding	
Asking for help	
Taking an hour out to go to the gym	
Not having sex with their husband	

What I have seen mums feel guilty about	What mums should feel guilty about
Buying the wrong baby sling	
Using a dummy	
Not using a dummy	
Their baby getting ill	
Their baby's head shape	
Not going to enough baby classes	
Using ready-made baby food	
Not using ready-made baby food	
Not asking for help	
Forgetting to do baby massage	
Wanting to be back at work	
Having to go back to work	
Feeling tired	
Not buying the right sippy cup	
Having a lie-in	
'Giving' their baby colic	

As a new mum every decision you make is important for your baby and everything you do to look after and love your baby is crucial. But you should not in any way be feeling guilty about the choices you make. Sadly, many mums I see, including my friends and myself, end up feeling guilty about things they are doing. I have no idea why we are programmed to do this – we seem to want to torture ourselves.

If you are loving and looking after your baby, you are doing enough. You have to be confident in the decisions you make and go forward, not look back with thoughts such as, 'If only I'd taken him to baby gym, he'd be rolling over by now.' That may sound crazy, but I assure you I hear that and similar guilt-infested comments a lot in clinic.

Feeling guilty undermines you as a mummy. Remember – you are the uber-goddess of mothering. You don't need to be beating yourself up about what you *should* be doing. Focus on what you *are* doing. And enjoy it. If you think you've done something 'wrong', then change it and keep going forwards.

If you have to ask for help with your baby because you find bathing him difficult, who cares? Nobody ever said you have to manage alone. You can't feel guilty about these things. If instinctively you feel you want a break from him on a Sunday morning when your other half is around to empty the nappy bin and feed him, do it. Don't drive yourself mad with the guilt.

Guilt is very wearing and very tiring and will stop you loving and basking in parenthood. I don't think there's time in the day when you're a parent to feel guilty. There are far too many other essential and fun things to be doing. Often the guilt is quite futile, especially when circumstances are out of your control. If you have to go back to work at some point, there is little point in feeling guilty about it. Easy for me to say, I know, and hard for you to do. But you have to try. I know, I've been there and done it – the 'Oh no, I just fed her a jar of baby food and there's no going back' cry. But life is a set of circumstances, some of which are in your control, and some of which aren't. Guilt undermines that all-knowing MUMMY-POWER, and you mustn't let it.

I am now going to make an awful gender stereotype comment based on zero scientific research, but on my own anecdotal experience: daddies don't seem to feel as guilty as us mums. And I admire and positively envy that! Men have the right attitude: make a decision and go with it. I don't hear daddies over-neurosing about the ridiculous minutiae of parenting. Perhaps it's because they usually remain with one foot in the working world, giving them more perspective on all this stuff. They are also not bombarded all the time with being told the right way of doing things or the wrong way. I don't know why, but they seem to have the guilt thing sussed: perhaps we all need to be a bit more manly? Well, sort of.

Sometimes other people spark off the guilt in you. I'm not sure why people do this, it can be a friend or, and I apologise, a healthcare professional. (You can read later on about how healthcare professionals don't always get the advice thing spot on). Guilt-inducers use phrases like:

- 'What you should have done ...'
- 'Didn't you know about ...'
- 'You've left it late ...'
- 'You've failed to ...'

Avoid, avoid, avoid. Run away and run fast! People who make you feel guilty about 'mistakes' you've made or your choices are not helpful to you and should not be your source of support. Find yourself a new friend. Find a new parenting forum. See a different GP. You need support and guidance as a mummy, not a telling off.

- Guilt undermines your mummy-power
- If someone makes you feel guilty regarding your parenting, avoid them
- Feeling guilty stops you enjoying baby

So remember, you are the expert and the only one your baby needs. You are the authority, the specialist and the doyenne on your little one. While you may need some help here and there, you've got this covered from day one. This is what mothers are for; you know how to bring up your baby, you've just got to trust yourself to do it.

Chapter 2

Sleep – What's Sleep?!

You probably didn't realise just how much you adored sleeping until your baby came along. Now it is most likely your number one, all-time favourite pastime. I am not embarrassed to confess it is mine.

Good sleep is vital for your baby to grow and develop and be happy. And it is just as essential for you to be rested and calm and happy. Happy mummy = happy baby and sleep is the cornerstone of happy parenting. That and a washing machine, of course.

What is definitely not vital is that you follow anyone else's idea of a sleeping plan. The only plan you need to follow is your baby's. There is no correct fool-proof way to sort out a baby's sleep, despite what people will claim. Yes, there are certainly some clever steps you can take to make the days and nights work, but the exact schedule you follow is only important to your little family, no one else.

I'm the type of person who needs a lot of sleep and I like to know when it's coming. Even when my babies were very young, I wanted predictability in my day. If you're the sort of person, like many of my patients, who very much go with the flow and are used to less structure, then clearly we're not going to have a matching timetable. But schedule or no schedule, what *everyone* needs is enough sleep, and to feel rested. That is the key to the big sleep conundrum: making it work for YOU. Not that your baby has a nap at exactly 11am but that you both feel rested. There is no magic formula or one-size-fits-all solution that will ensure your baby gets a full night's sleep. You simply have to trust your instinct and learn from your baby what is right.

Sleeping through the night seems to be this panacea all new parents are striving for. Of course that is understandable, but please remember it is not an indicator of your parenting skills. Learning to sleep through is a natural process babies have been doing for millennia. It is not a test of your parenting prowess – you are simply there to guide your baby on her way with some clever tricks. You are not a failure if your baby is not instantly sleeping through the night. The perfect ingredients to make a baby a 'good' sleeper are made up of:

- Your baby's temperament – 70 per cent.
- Luck – 5 per cent.
- Common sense and a few practical approaches – 25 per cent.

I can illustrate my exceedingly scientific formula using my own kids as an example. I have two children. They have the same parents who used the same approaches both times. One slept through the night consistently at 10 weeks old. One slept through the night consistently at two-and-a-half years old.

Good sleep habits and practical approaches encourage sleep but they are only part of the equation. Be honest about this with yourself, so you are realistic and you don't feel guilty if your baby doesn't sleep all night at three months old. This is not a one-size-fits-all routine that will guarantee slumber-filled nights. This is just honest, realistic advice to help you on to the right path.

- Keep calm (difficult when you're shattered)
- Trust your instinct
- Very quickly you will become the sleep expert

Coping with sleeplessness in the first few weeks

In the early days, by which I mean the first five or six weeks, but possibly even the first three months, tiredness and sleepless nights are a fact of life and, quite frankly, you just have to accept that. Brutal, I know, but I'm not in the business of making false promises and that's the harsh reality.

New parents are sleep deprived: that isn't news and you won't be any different. No babies are born knowing the difference between night and day. They've been living in a bubble for nine months, so it takes a while to get used to life on Earth. They need feeding often – 2–3-hourly, including overnight – and the sooner you get used to that, the easier you'll find life. You have to accept that's the way it is and go with the flow. The very zombified flow. (See Chapter 5 for more on this …)

Being pragmatic about sleeplessness and learning to cope with the short-term tiredness means you will keep calm and enjoy your baby. Now is the time to have very little expectation: this is not forever and you'll soon be out the other side. At some point in a few months you will once again know the pleasure of being intimate with your duvet for a *whole* night: you just have to be patient.

Of course, there'll be some smug mummy in your antenatal group with a robot-baby who sleeps peacefully for eight-hour stretches, while yours can't even cope with doing two hours straight. Well, I promise you, she is the anomaly, not you. And knowing competitive mummies, as I do, chances are that sleep tale is rather exaggerated. There is absolutely no point in comparing your baby's sleep pattern to others because it will only cause you panic, stress and make you feel inferior. Sleeplessness is normal in the early days – your baby and your exhaustion is no different to anyone else's. You are a super-mum whether you've had 14 hours' sleep or 14 minutes'. (By the way, no mother has *ever* had 14 hours' sleep.)

Being a mummy expert at this stage involves coping with the sleeplessness, not stressing about it. The skill here is self-preservation. Managing with sleepless nights is one of the hardest things to get used to as a new parent and that is why us parents talk about sleep *all* the time. Sleep deprivation is a bit like being run over by a 5-tonne truck on your way to work every day. It is a big strain on you and your other half, and you've got to acknowledge that and come up with some sensible strategies to handle it.

Once you have experienced a few sleepless nights, you will know why people describe insomnia as a form of torture. You'll feel completely peculiar during the day with anxiety, stress and nausea: it is not nice, but remember this is a phase and every other new parent feels the same.

I try not to disagree with patients as a rule, but I once argued with a new mum who was convinced she was seriously ill two months after her baby was born because of her severe nausea and headaches. She was sleeping in stretches of two hours at a time, but couldn't believe it was merely tiredness that was affecting her body so much. We did blood tests and other investigations that proved normal, yet I still couldn't convince her. It was only once her sleeping improved drastically and the physical symptoms literally vanished that she could see what a profound effect the fatigue was having on her body. Be warned: do not underestimate the crazy powers of sleep deprivation!

In the early days, unless you have someone helping you, you have to learn to manage with little sleep and I guarantee you will. All mummies do. It is just one of our expert powers. For a few weeks, sleeping two or three hours at a time is going to be normal, and so is feeling like you've been bashed over the head with a mallet. Weirdly enough, you will get used to it. Keep calm, listen to your body and concentrate at this stage on self-preservation. Your baby's sleeping will get better and better as she gets older: while the first few weeks drag by in a haze, be a little bit savvy about handling the whole thing. Some strategies that may help:

- Work in shifts if there's another adult around: you don't both need to be up with your baby. One adult per baby is a good-enough ratio.
- Do not watch your baby sleep (I have spent years doing this) – it may be cute, but it is a waste of your own precious sleeping time.
- Grab sleep in the day when you can, even 30 minutes is worth it. If someone gives you this opportunity, take it immediately before they have time to change their mind.
- Don't go crazy with the coffee to keep yourself awake because if the chance to grab 40 winks arises, you'll be too wired to take it.
- Don't compare your baby to other babies – sleeping is not a competitive sport.
- Remember, this will probably only be for a few weeks and every day and night gets better and better.

The more you let yourself sleep in the first few weeks, the better you will feel: this will give you all the expert mumpower that you need. Then you will have the energy to think about shrewd strategies to encourage your baby's long-term sleeping habits. I find a lot of 'bad' sleep habits have come about because mums are too tired to address them. So I have them telling me: 'We were desperate to get her to sleep so we just rocked her – and now we always need to rock her.' If you are careful to protect your own sleep in the early days, when it comes to it you'll have the mental and physical energy to instil good, consistent sleep habits in your baby. And the zombie days will soon be over.

Should I put my baby into a routine to help her sleep?

Routine is another word, like perineum, dilate and poo ,that you hardly ever use before you get pregnant, and then once that baby pops out, it feels like you say it *all* the time:

- 'Is your baby in a routine?'
- 'My baby doesn't really have a routine.'
- 'The routine's gone out the window.'
- 'You have to have a routine.'
- 'I hate the routine.'

So the big question every mummy wants to know is, do you *need* a routine for your baby?

The answer to this question comes from you and only you. It is neither right nor wrong to put your baby into a routine. There are no rules. No guidelines. There is an absolute mountain of good and bad stuff written about babies' sleep and what you must do to be a successful parent. The only thing you *must* do is follow your instinct. While there is plenty of opinion about what people think works and helps babies to be good sleepers, the truth is that it is an entirely personal choice and hugely, totally dependent on what your own sleeping beauty is like.

Routine means sticking to the same times each day for feeds, sleeps and activities. It gives you a lot of predictability, like any timetable, and goes some way to help you plan the day and night. Some people will claim it makes for more settled, happier babies. Well, I look after a lot of babies who grow up in madness and mayhem, and they are also settled and happy. A routine is not essential. It works for some babies and some mummies.

Instilling a routine does *not* guarantee you will create a genius baby, a sleeping robot or have a perfectly joyful parenting experience. It simply means you have a time-table in your day. Many women find it makes life easier to have some structure in the day and know that feeding times and nap times are in place. That certainly goes some way to making you feel in control. But it is certainly not a one-size-fits-all approach. Many people don't want rigid structure, and a lot of mummies I have met feel the routine ends up controlling *them*, which is not good. You've got to trust yourself on this one.

I know from the mums I look after that routine is not for everyone. I think you know whether you are the kind of person who needs a schedule and structure. I definitely am and I tried with both my children to fit them into a routine, with varying degrees of success. For many mums I see, set nap times are an absolute pain, and feeding 'on demand' is far preferable to any set schedule. Their babies are as settled and chilled as any timetabled baby, probably because the mums feel settled and chilled and, therefore, in control. A calm mum has a calm baby, whether that baby is micro-managed or not.

One of the biggest parenting secrets is that, actually, the majority of babies have their own little pattern and fall into it naturally. Whether you think you want a routine or not, your baby will naturally have her own and you simply need to follow that lead.

Be careful not to try following someone else's timetable as it stops you from watching and learning from your own baby. Rather than listening to yourself and your baby, you're following someone else's rules, and that will undermine your own expertise.

Diluting mummy-power is not good! You have to start to trust yourself on this as a great foundation for your whole parenting life. Sleep is a massive area for trusting your instinct, and learning from yourself and your baby. The only bona fide sleep guru for your baby is YOU. There is no point trying to implement a lunchtime nap if it doesn't fit in with your baby's inherent rhythm or the fact that you want to be out at lunchtime. That is setting yourself up for failure: if you are going to follow a rigid pattern, it has to fit in primarily with your baby's own patterns. Babies are not robots and it doesn't make sense that they should all follow a dictated timetable: some sleep more, some sleep less, some sleep in the morning, some sleep over lunchtime. Routine or no routine, watch and learn from your baby and trust yourself to become her sleep expert.

Right from the start, from the crazy, hazy zombie days, if you want a structure then look for your baby's patterns and follow her lead. If she always seems to have a long sleep in the morning, encourage that and continue to consistently put her down for that sleep. If that's naturally when she's tired, working together will formulate the routine that is destined to succeed. If she always seems shattered after the physical excesses of a liquid lunch, put her down for a nap then. Watch for those cues that tell you she is tired and go with it. Instinct, instinct, instinct comes before rules, rules, rules.

Both of my kids were evening sleepers right from the first few weeks; I did not implement this at all, we just noticed they did it. Even by 10 days my son (the one who took more than two years to sleep through the night, by the way) would consistently sleep in his cot through the evening. It was a natural pattern and I got lucky. After six weeks with my first child, I was so confident of her evening routine, I even *SHOCK, HORROR* got a babysitter (well, my dad to be honest) one evening so I could go out: don't be envious, I went to Tesco. I didn't instil this evening sleeping in my children, it happened naturally and I followed their lead. Once we noticed that pattern, and it seemed like a good one, we encouraged it and made sure every evening we put them down to sleep the same way, to promote their own slumber habits.

A lot of my patients use a diary to work out sleep patterns, and gradually even after four or five weeks you may see a routine developing. In fact, when you do this, it is amazing to see your baby's own schedule developing, which more than likely will be similar to other babies of the same age. The key word there is 'similar', not *identical*. You have then created your very own unique baby routine, written and directed by you, the new member of the sleep-guru club.

- Listen to your baby
- Trust yourself as a sleep expert
- If routine feels right, it is right

Consistency is more important than routine

No one has the foolproof answer to getting a baby to sleep through the night.

No method will guarantee your baby will sleep through but you can be savvy and smart with consistency to help your baby on her way. Being predictable with your mummy messages encourages good sleep habits in your little one and will send her on the right path to a night's sleep. Consistency is like laying a foundation, and it seems to have worked for centuries.

While I would never advise a mum to put her baby into a routine or not, I would always suggest being consistent. Babies like predictability and respond very well to it. In much the same way you have your own little ways of doing things – making a cup of tea just how you like it, plumping up the pillows in a certain way – babies like their own patterns too. Humans love pattern recognition – it makes us feel settled and secure to know what we're doing and when.

Being consistent with your own bedtime and night-time customs encourages your baby's own sleep habits to fall into place. This is exactly what GPs like myself do to help adults who have sleeping problems: we encourage patients to fix a consistent, winding-down, bedtime blueprint. And it works.

For centuries mums have put their babies to bed with a pattern of lights down and bath, boob, bed or bath, bottle, bed (b-b-b). This has nothing to do with cleanliness and everything to do with consistent slumber-time messages: it's our way of saying, 'Right young lady, it's time for bed because I need to watch EastEnders.'

Every night, whether you can be bothered or not, stick to that consistent approach: I find many of my mummies do this whether they are 'routine types' or not. Your baby knows where she stands and you're signalling the start of bedtime.

You can start this even within the first few weeks. It doesn't have to be the b-b-b way – use whatever works for you. You might read the same book, sing the same song, give a little massage. Make it pretty straightforward: that's probably why the b-b-b routine works because it's cheap and simple and repeatable every night, wherever you are. It's not *what* you're doing that's important, it's that you're doing it *every* time to signal bedtime.

You can do this at 7pm or 11pm or whatever time is 'bedtime' in your house: that is entirely up to you (believe me, there will be some days when you want to do this at 5pm!) What matters to create the good sleep habits is the practical repeated pattern of what you do. So the nighty-night message gets through loud and clear.

The same consistent approach is also key during the night to teach your baby, gently, that you want to be under your duvet, not cooing at her. Always make sure night feels like night and that it is different from the bright, fun-filled day. Make night-feeds quiet and calm, with the lights low: instinctively that makes sense to any mummy, of course. If your baby needs settling during the night, which is perfectly normal, stick to the same night-time approach every time. You are not going to get it wrong: however you find to settle her overnight, stick to it and be consistent each time so she learns the beauty of calm, slumber-filled nights.

- Listen to your instinct
- Consistency is a great mummy expert tool
- Trust yourself to do this

Settling to sleep

You and your baby are now laying down sleep patterns that will probably stick. If you teach your baby over the first few months that she needs some sort of comforter to fall asleep, then she may always need that. I have no problem with babies falling asleep by being rocked or by using dummies, muslins, boobs, nightlights, white noise simulators, and even cuddly Daleks (I see it all in my job), as long as you realise that your baby may become reliant on that sleep aid. Now that might be fine for you; it was fine for me with my muslin-addict babies. I just want you to be aware so you can make choices that work for your family. I am definitely not saying *don't* use a sleep aid, it's more of a gentle warning that is worth heeding: I'm saying choose wisely as the comforter may be around for a while and your baby's dependency on it may surprise or disappoint you when it happens. (See also Chapter 4 on crying and soothing.)

Some babies do naturally grow out of sleep aids very easily and almost accidentally within their first year. You hear a lot of mums saying, for example, 'She just stopped wanting a dummy.' But just in case your darling doesn't grow out of her sleep aid, let's be savvy.

So, for example, breastfeeding your baby to sleep is

fine, as long as you're prepared to do that for the next few months. There are no detrimental effects to this other than it will sometimes be a right pain for you. You may not feel like it now, but there will come a time when you actually quite fancy going out for an evening, and if you're the only one that can breastfeed your baby to sleep you're trapped! A sleep aid has to work for everyone so consider long-term workable ones.

Of course the first few weeks are all over the place: your baby will be sleeping a bit here, a bit there, falling asleep on you, on Grandma, on the postman – anyone, it doesn't really matter. But be aware that you are already creating sleep associations, so as often as you can, avoid the inconvenient ones. If you don't want to be rocking your baby to sleep every night for a year, my advice is don't start. Remember what I said about consistency? Patterns start to stick quickly. While I hate the expression 'training' when referring to sleep, you are effectively conditioning your baby to associate sleep with certain things. So make those things easy and convenient for you: muslins, dummies, thumbs and lullabies are all convenient.

Time after time after time I see mums caught with inconvenient sleep aids really by accident because they started using something and it got stuck. This often happens through sheer exhaustion; that's why I started off this chapter by saying you have to prioritise your own sleep so you have the energy to sort out your baby's. Being stuck with an inconvenient sleep aid leads to unnecessary mummy-guilt and a faff later on when you try to get rid of it, so be wise with your initial choices.

Of course there will be times when your baby falls asleep on you, or on your boob. And of course in the first few weeks there'll be times you'll need to rock her to sleep, and there'll be fraught occasions later on when she'll sleep on you. That is completely normal and natural; no mummy would ever suggest you didn't cuddle and soothe your baby when she needs it. I'm just gently saying don't let it be her consistent sleep-association unless you're 100 per cent happy with that for the long haul.

If you want your baby to fall asleep on her own from the outset, watch for her cues and you can start this pretty early on. Learn from her and your instinct. Not all babies *need* a sleep aid: trust your instinct to know when she is tired and put her down in your chosen predictable way. She may settle solo or you may need to use a dummy or a gentle pat to sleep. Whatever it is that you choose, stick with it and be consistent for all sleepy-time associations.

- Start how you mean to go on: for example, if you don't want to use a dummy, don't start
- Choose convenient sleep aids
- Make sure it's not just you that can settle baby

There is one rule

We know from research and proper science that the safest way for your baby to sleep is on her back in her own cot or crib, with her feet at the foot of the cot so she can't wriggle under covers. This is not negotiable. This has been shown to prevent cot death in babies, which thankfully is a very rare occurrence anyway, but now even rarer since the introduction of this essential rule.

Once babies get to five or six months old they often start to roll over in their sleep, and you will find them in all manner of positions around the cot. This is fine, as, just like adults, they start to toss and turn in their sleep. You do not need to keep repositioning them on to their back once they're rolling around, but you still need to be careful to make sure they can't end up trapped under the covers. This is why many parents opt for infant sleeping-bags which keep babies warm, without any danger of suffocation.

What is a normal amount of sleep?

You will know if your baby is getting enough sleep because she will seem okay and you will feel fine. You will just know. No signs, no instructions, no rules. It will just feel right for you and her.

There are no laws that dictate when a baby must sleep through the night: most won't before three months and most will by a year, but there is a huge spectrum of babies in between. It is not a competitive sport, and when your baby sleeps through is not a reflection of your mummy skills. There's so much over-egging of sleeping by competitive mums: ignore the crazy crowd, just listen to yourself and your baby.

All babies will nap during the day but again there is no normal. In the beginning, babies nap a lot, for the majority of the day on and off, with one or two long naps and a few power-naps. It's a fine life being a newborn isn't it? Around the six-month mark, your typical textbook baby will be doing about three or four hours of napping as well as her night-time stint. As she gets older, she'll nap less in the day until she's a year old when she'll probably have one chunky nap of about two hours. This is only what baby-average does and there are plenty of variations on this theme; your baby may be completely different, and still perfectly normal.

What to do when things don't go smoothly

Many babies just get better and better at sleeping until that magic moment when you wake up in the morning and realise you've been in bed all night. Bliss. But for plenty of babies there will be times when it doesn't go smoothly and you won't feel like you're winning with the sleep. This is a fact of life as a parent. Dealing with this is like dealing with sleep right in the beginning: it takes a calm, consistent approach. That is very easy for me to say and very difficult for you to do in the thick of exhaustion. It takes a lot of strength and mummy-power to keep going and try different strategies to get your baby's sleep on track. You *will* find an answer, it may just take time. An honest action plan for managing sleep setbacks:

- Go back to basics – stick to the bedtime signals and the strict night-time quiet cues. Sometimes in the haze of exhaustion, you may have been lax on these, so make sure you're doing them.
- Stay consistent – if you're trying to settle your baby in her room, don't walk around the house with her sometimes and other times not. Stick to the same consistent message that tells her you're not taking any nonsense and you expect her to be asleep.
- You may not be the answer – us mummies tend to think we are the only ones who can settle our babies. Dads (or grannies, or sisters) are there to be utilised. Other adults are often fabulous at night-time settling as they don't smell of milk (usually) and their less-frazzled, calmer approach may do the trick. Go on! Let Dad try for a few nights in a row.
- Whatever solution you try give it time to bed in and be consistent with your effort (no point trying a leaving-to-cry method if you actually can't see it through). No solution will work overnight; it will take a while to see a result.
- Only try one potential solution at a time.
- Do not ever think of yourself as a failure – babies have setbacks in their sleep and that is not your fault.
- Give it time and be patient – whether your baby's sleep is unsettled for a night or a month, it is not forever. Things will get better, and you have to take each night as it comes.

If your baby's sleep hasn't turned out how you'd hoped, you will hear of countless different strategies that people try: leaving to cry, patting, shushing, walking in and out, and a thousand other complicated methods. There are plenty of these tried-and-tested ways that can work to salvage sleep. I purposely say *can*, because there are certainly no promises, and all babies are different. There is not one solution for everyone, so you may have to try a few in turn before one works for you.

Equally, the solution to your sleep woes may actually be home-grown from your instinct, rather than a complex plan. If you think something might work, try it: you have nothing to lose and a night's sleep to gain. You can't go wrong. I got fed up and frustrated trying difficult strategies to help my son sleep through the night; in the end, I had a hunch that although he was just two, maybe he'd sleep through if I put him in a toddler-bed rather than a cot. And as if by magic, I've not heard a peep from him overnight since.

A friend of mine had recently been struggling with her nine-month-old waking in the middle of the night and needing settling, and she was finding it tough doing the leaving-to-cry thing. The shushing-patting approach didn't seem to work either. So she had a go at settling him by talking to him through the monitor: she only tried this because one night she was just too tired to get out of bed. And guess what? It worked. No clever methodology, just simple shushing down the radio waves and that was that. He was back to sleep without her leaving the comfort of her bed. The solution may be just as simple for you. Listen to yourself. Things will get better, it just takes a calm, sensible sleep expert: you.

Have I got this right?

It doesn't actually matter how you have sorted out your baby's sleep, as long as you have sorted it. If you feel all right and instinct tells you your baby is fine then you've got it right. Getting it 'right' doesn't have to mean your baby sleeps 12 hours straight: it means whatever it takes for you all to feel good.

All babies are different from the point of view of sleep and your pattern won't end up the same as mine or the girl next door. It doesn't matter because there is no written law to follow. I was very comfortable with my evening-sleeping babies so I could watch low-grade TV and flop on the couch. Close friends of mine were just as contented having their babies with them in the evening for months, whether baby was on their boob or in the bouncer. I wasn't right, they weren't wrong. We're all different. You just need to be sure it's working for YOU. I always felt I could cope with getting up in the night because I'd had an evening to myself to mentally relax. You may be different.

A fabulous mum I look after, with quite frankly the most high-powered job ever, still wakes up three times a night with her one-year-old to feed her. The baby doesn't need to feed because she's a good size and eats well in the day. Mummy knows, as I do, her baby is waking up for comfort. I was exhausted just hearing about it.

'Aren't you both tired?' I asked her.

'At the moment we're coping, and this works for us. I'm used to it now.'

Now many mums, like me, would have been shattered holding down a stressful job with such broken sleep. But for this family, and other families I have come across, it works for them. For now, this feels right to her, and instinctively she is comfortable doing it. She knows she'll have to sort this out at some point, but not until she's ready. And right now for her, waking up is preferable to trying to break the habit. Experts and textbooks would say she is 'wrong' to do this, but she isn't. It works for them at the moment and it doesn't really matter about anyone else.

- Keep calm
- Trust your instinct
- Listen to the baby expert: YOU

Chapter 3
Feeding – Your Baby, Your Business

There is only one rule: you have to feed your baby. That is all. Breastfeeding mothers are wonderful, loving, dedicated mummies who should be proud of themselves. Equally, bottle-feeding mothers are wonderful, loving, dedicated mummies who should be proud of themselves.

If you are breastfeeding your baby, you should quite rightly feel proud and contented. It's a fantastic thing to do, for both of you, and deserves recognition and pride. If you are bottle-feeding your baby, sadly you are made to feel rather different ... so let's have a think about what's really going on.

It is a crazy fact of life in today's world of parenting that whatever I write in a chapter about feeding is going to upset someone. In the swamp of parenting guidelines and pseudo-expertise that bombards mummies in the 21st century, there is far, far too much written about feeding babies. I have been in the parent-world for more than a decade and I am still amazed by the sheer volume of material that is produced on feeding. A tiny quantity of this stuff is real, scientific-based advice. The rest should be filed under C for claptrap.

How you feed your baby is only one person's business – YOURS. Every single person will have an opinion on whether you breastfeed or bottle-feed, but the fact of the matter is, the only opinion that counts is yours. If you want to bottle-feed your baby or if you want to breastfeed, it is entirely up to you, and only you. Mothers spend far too much time feeling guilty, confused or upset about their feeding choice and it is quite wrong.

We now have books written entirely on breastfeeding, blogs on breastfeeding, campaign groups for breastfeeding mothers. The internet, advice columns, newspapers, Facebook groups are full to the brim of pages dedicated to breastfeeding: why you should do it, why it's best, why you're a better mother if you choose it. There are women who have made a career out of breastfeeding and extolling its virtues – well, that's fine, good luck to you dears, you're doing a fab job. But quite honestly, the world doesn't need to hear about it.

However you choose to feed your baby or, to be more realistic, however the feeding pans out (because it isn't always a *choice*), you have to stick with your decision and enjoy it. It is not, I repeat *not*, a measure of how good a mother you are. As a mother and a doctor I am sick and tired of women being made to feel guilty about their feeding method. Why should mothers have to justify this to doctors, friends, bloggers and random strangers in cafes? All mothers are heroes, not just breastfeeding mothers. Being a good mother is about *all* the things you do for your baby, and feeding one way doesn't make you a failure.

The obsession with breastfeeding as a measure of superiority or ability is damaging and degrading to women. As a mum, you do what is best for your baby and you do not have to justify that to anybody. You will hear people talk about the breast versus bottle debate – and in reality this is exactly how it is for many mothers I see. They are torn between what they think they want to do for their baby, what they can cope with and what everyone else is telling them to do. It can become a big mess of emotion, frustration and tears, which I have seen countless times in clinic. You have to make sure you and your baby are number one, and as long as you're feeding your baby with either a boob or a bottle, or perhaps both, you're doing just fine.

There is far too much discussion, ridiculous non-scientific information and (as I have witnessed many times) dangerous phoney-guidelines that can put babies and mums at risk. The fact of the matter is you have to feed a baby somehow, and you must not let yourself be bombarded by all the crazy feeding talk out there. Trust your instinct and your own desire to do the best thing for your baby, and you won't go wrong with feeding. Don't allow yourself to be fazed and browbeaten by those around you (including, and I apologise, healthcare professionals). Be confident in your choice and go with it. It is really difficult to keep calm but try. You are a super-mamma and that has nothing to do with your boobs. Or any other part of your body for that matter.

I am not giving you permission to bottle-feed or breast-feed because, quite frankly, it is none of my business. I am giving you permission to make your own way, free from guilt.

- Keep calm
- Trust yourself
- You are a feeding expert

You don't need to apologise

As a GP, I have to ask all new mothers how they are feeding their babies at the six-week check. More often than not, if a patient of mine is not breastfeeding she apologises to me. Teary, sad and guilt-ridden, I have mums in my surgery saying to me, 'I'm sorry Dr Cannon, I'm not breastfeeding.' At times, I'm not ashamed to say, this has even made me teary.

You don't need to apologise to anyone about how you feed your baby. Bottle-feeding mothers are not second-class mothers who need to apologise. Just like breastfeeding mums shouldn't have to apologise for getting their boobs out in the library (as long as it's to feed the baby), bottle-feeding mothers should never feel they have to apologise. A sample of the many reasons mums tell me they're not breastfeeding:

- 'I don't like it.'
- 'I don't want to.'

- 'I never even considered doing it.'
- 'It's not working.'
- 'It went wrong.'
- 'I wanted to but I couldn't.'

Quite honestly, none of these reasons are unjustifiable or a reason to apologise. Some believe that every woman can breastfeed, but I really don't think that this is the case. In fact, I hands-down refuse to acknowledge that every woman can breastfeed. It just doesn't make sense given all the mums I've seen who have tried so hard and failed. Women who really wanted to feed but physically couldn't.

Of course, it's natural and our bodies are designed for it, but bodies don't always work to the grand evolutionary plan. Have a think back to labour: you go into labour and your cervix starts to dilate. At least it's supposed to dilate, but it doesn't for all women. What about all those cervixes that don't dilate, so the baby has to be delivered by Caesarean section? Midwives don't say to those women: 'Listen love, you really should be using your vagina for the birth of the baby, so we won't be offering you a Caesarean.' That would be crazy, right? It might be the most natural way, but it doesn't always work in reality. Some boobs just don't work well, just like some cervixes. The end. No apology necessary. You don't apologise for your cervix if you have a Caesarean, so don't apologise for your boobs either.

Many women feel they don't make milk, or it dries up, or breastfeeding is very painful or even just uncomfortable. No one can tell you you're wrong and you have to persist because that is the natural way. Mammary glands, like babies, don't all follow the textbooks and do what they're *supposed* to do. And that is fine. It's disappointing often for women who give up breastfeeding, but it's reality and it happens often. It can even change with each child: I had one baby who was easy-peasy to feed while the other one definitely hadn't read the instruction manual.

Dictating that *every woman can feed if she wants to* leads to feelings of failure and unnecessary guilt, which is really, really unfair to an already upset mummy. The other rather massive issue to address is that boobs don't work alone. They are usually attached to a woman (unless I missed any latest innovations) who has a mind and a heart and feelings. And breastfeeding might not work for that mind or heart or feelings: if you don't 'want' to breastfeed or if you don't like it, I really don't think anyone has a right to ignore that and force you into it. Some women genuinely find breastfeeding makes them miserable and I really don't think it's fair you have to apologise for that.

- Keep calm
- This is your choice
- You do not need to apologise

But you're a doctor, surely you believe breast is best?

I do. I 100 per cent believe breast milk is the best thing to feed a baby: taking all other factors *out* of the equation (i.e. the mummy) and simply looking at breast milk versus formula milk, we know breastfeeding is the optimal way to feed a baby. This is undisputed medical information.

Breastfeeding is rightly recommended as the first choice by the World Health Organisation, the Department of Health and all medical establishments. There are scientifically proven benefits of breastfeeding as breast milk fully meets a baby's dietary needs. In countries where clean water is a rarity, it is positively lifesaving. Thankfully, that doesn't apply to the UK. But it still has benefits: it has antibodies, it is packed with the right nutritional ingredients and don't forget it's *free* – a virtue not extolled enough in my opinion!

We know breastfed babies have fewer allergies, tummy infections and ear infections. Some of the other claims about breastfeeding are rather overplayed/complete codswallop: for example, breastfed babies are not superior intellectually, nor are they closer to their mothers and they are not guaranteed to be happier than their bottle-fed peers.

So yes, breast is best when you are comparing one milk to another, not taking into account the delivery method or availability. But that's not realistic because, as I pointed out, it's not always readily available and breasts don't work in isolation of a thinking, feeling mummy. So I have two important additions to the *breast is best* mantra:

1. Breastfeeding is not always best for mummy.
2. Formula is not harmful.

While breast milk may be the best option for your baby, if breastfeeding isn't actually working then we can't say it's best. If it's making you miserable or ill, then that clearly outweighs the advantages of the milk itself and breast is no longer best. It's a balancing act. Let's be sensible about it.

Recently, a patient ended up in hospital with her newborn after he lost 20 per cent of his birthweight. She had wanted to breastfeed and when her baby was born she had breastfed him straight away and continued to do so. But she had a feeling it wasn't going right and that her baby wasn't perky enough. So she sought advice in the end from three different outlets during one week. Everyone, including her local midwife, told her to persist because breastfeeding was *best*. She asked about top-ups and was told, no, *breast is best*. So she followed the mantra, not her instinct. But on day 11 her instinct took over, thankfully, and she took her baby to A&E. He was admitted to hospital with dehydration having lost weight; the mum had been led away from her own maternal instinct that something was wrong by the misguided notion that breast is best in all circumstances. This can be dangerous advice. Breast is best, but not at the expense of sense.

While breast milk is superior, formula is not harmful. Bottle-feeding has never been proven to be detrimental. If formula is like cake, breast milk is the cake with the icing. Cake is great; icing on cake is that extra bit better. Icing is not for everyone and not everyone can do it. Breastfeeding is not for everyone and not everyone can do it.

In an ideal world, we'd all breastfeed our babies and formula wouldn't be necessary, but we don't live in a textbook world and no mummy should be feeling guilty about that.

- Above all else, trust your instinct
- Keep calm
- Feeling guilty is not an option

Right. So now I've got that off my chest, so to speak, let's deal with some of the important practicalities of feeding.

It's all gone tits up but I want to carry on

Excellent. If you want to carry on breastfeeding and it is going wrong, then you need to quickly find yourself some help. And you need to find yourself good-quality assistance: therein lies the problem, as it's hard to find good help.

Breastfeeding advice is generally confusing, conflicting and we all give you different opinions. I'm sorry about this, but you need to be warned. Time and time again I hear this, so you need to be savvy. Potentially a midwife, a breastfeeding counsellor, a health visitor or a GP may be able to help you, but you have to find a good one. GPs have little or no training in breastfeeding – the only reason I know about it is because I did it: it certainly isn't something I learnt about at medical school.

The best person to help you may actually not be a so-called 'expert', but may be a friend who's done it and gone through problems, or someone you know with an older baby who might know some tricks of the trade. Be wary of people who say only their way is right: it may be you have to try a few things before you feel settled with it. Try one solution at a time, so you can see what is helping. It is very tempting when you're desperate to sort things out, to throw in all the ammunition at once: don't, because you won't know which strategy is really working. Be a bit patient; yes, I know it's not easy.

Breastfeeding doesn't come instantly to every mummy, and taking a few weeks to get to grips with it is normal for plenty of women who go on to breastfeed for years easily and happily. Keep calm. If you want to do it, you will find your own solution: don't panic if it takes some time. Your instinct is still key. If you do get some advice and it seems wrong, move on. Trust yourself at all times.

At any point when you are struggling, if you feel your baby may be not feeding enough, do not ignore that. Get your baby weighed and checked over for dehydration by a healthcare professional as soon as you are concerned. This is vital. It may be that he is not taking enough milk and while you're still learning, you need to give him a top-up of formula. This is not a problem at all. Many of my patients use top-up bottles in this way to ensure their baby is adequately hydrated and fed. This takes the pressure off you when you are struggling and can ensure he's safe.

An honest action plan to get breastfeeding back on track:

1. Think about the 'latch': how baby sucks on your nipple affects how much he gets and how you feel during feeding. This may mean trying different positions, different cushions or even in the beginning asking someone to help position his head while you learn the knack

2. Nipple shields, nipple inverters and nipple creams are all worth a try if you think they may help. Try one thing at a time and see for yourself if they work for YOU. People have strong opinions on nipple shields but if they help you to feed comfortably, that's all that matters

3. Make it easier for yourself: do not try and feed surrounded by thousands of onlookers while you try to preserve your modesty. Stick to feeding at home while you learn the basics

4. Relax yourself to relax him. When breastfeeding is hard, each feed is a source of stress and anguish. Ask Dad or Granny to sit with you to keep you calm, or put the radio on to distract you from your worry

5. Only ask one person for help at a time and try each solution in turn. If it's not working, move on to a new solution after a few days. I see panicked new parents trying every potential solution at every feed and it doesn't work

6. Give yourself time: it can take a while to master the skills, even if it is natural

It's all gone tits up and I want to stop

If you want to stop breastfeeding, think about it carefully first. I always get mums to do this before they completely give up, just as a safety net. This is a bit of self-preservation I've learnt from years of seeing mums stop and regret it. It's very difficult to return to breastfeeding once you cut down, and your milk supply reduces, so you have to be sure this is the route you want to take. Remember that business about being comfortable with your choice? Will you be happy sitting with the mummy-gang, all boobies-galore out in Starbucks and you're the one warming up formula? The reason I want you to think about this is because it really can end up mattering to you.

I see plenty of mums who give up breastfeeding and then spend the next year reliving it and how it went wrong. This is partly regret, partly guilt and partly feeling like a failure. You can give up whenever it feels right for you, but just slow down and think first so you are comfortable with your decision. Unfortunately, mummies who stop breast-feeding because it didn't 'work' do experience guilt and some sadness so you have to be prepared for that.

Think about whether or not you have to give up completely: while we always harp on about the breastfeeders versus the bottle-feeders, there's a very happy camp of mums who are mixed-feeding, giving a combination of breast milk and formula. So many of my patients do this really well, either on purpose or by chance. A young mummy I know did this recently, as she realised (with no advice by the way, simply instinct) that she had less milk in the evening. So she uses formula in the evening, and breastfeeding the rest of the time. She's happy she's still breastfeeding and her baby is settled. That was her compromise. She calls herself a 'breastfeeder' because she is one. She sits with her antenatal crowd breastfeeding. She doesn't hide the fact she gives a bottle, she just doesn't see it as a big deal. If you ask breastfeeding mothers if they also give a bottle, a surprising number will say yes.

Mixed-feeding mummies keep their options open and seem to have it sussed. Happily breastfeeding while at the same time bottle-feeding is a real choice not to be dismissed: and it can be a good halfway house if you think you want to stop. It gives you time to think, without giving up too quickly and regretting it. Especially as there's not really any going back once you stop.

If you have given it careful thought, and you are sure you want to stop breastfeeding, then that is absolutely fine. No guilt. No failure. It is your choice, and your choice alone. The only rule is that it is important to stop breastfeeding slowly, so your breasts do not become engorged and sore. You should drop a feed every few days, so your breasts gradually produce less milk. If you no longer want to put your baby to the breast, you can wean production down by expressing instead.

Are there rules on formula?

No, thankfully not really. There isn't really a huge amount to know about formula that isn't written on the side of the tin. Of course you have to make it up according to the instructions with cooled, boiled water and never ever be tempted to add more scoops than you're supposed to.

Start with the quantity for your baby's age written on the side of the tin and take it from there. He may need more, he may need less. You won't get it wrong if you are following signs from him and your own instinct. There is not an exact quantity that is right for every baby. It is completely up to your individual baby, and what he fancies drinking. This can change feed-to-feed sometimes, so you have to go with the flow. Literally.

All formula milks are the same. I'm pretty sure that's why they are called formula. I've noticed over the past few years that some formulas have become more fashionable than others: I think this is based on the assumption that a higher price tag means a cooler product, but I really don't believe that's true for baby milk. Whatever your baby takes to is the right one. Occasionally, people find they need to change formula (see page 127) but this is unusual.

If one real rule is allowed to sneak into the feeding chapter, it is that you must be sterilising all bottles, teats and feeding paraphernalia. Whether you use good old-fashioned sterilising tablets, or some marvellous high-tech contraption, it doesn't matter. You just gotta do it. This is sound, medical advice that prevents your little one getting nasty infections his immune system can't cope with.

There are certainly some super-duper bottles to buy nowadays, but no bottle or teat has ever been scientifically proven to be better than any other. Start with one that is minimal-faff and looks easy to clean, and experiment for yourself. There is no right or wrong here: if your baby is happy with his bottles and comfortable glugging the milk, you've got it right. There is a vast array of bottle paraphernalia but rest assured you need very little of it. Yes, it might be nice to have a bottle warmer but I always warmed bottles in a jug of hot water, which certainly did the trick. Some companies are set up on the flawed premise that 'parent' is a synonym for 'bottomless pit of cash' and love to sell you things you really don't need. This is true for the entire parenting arena, but particularly around feeding bits and bobs. Just be a bit sceptical before you part with your hard-earned cash.

Should I be expressing?

Expressing milk is another great area for overly abundant, pseudo-advice and meddling! It is really up to you and your lifestyle if you want or need to express breast milk. I think it's very handy to express milk and store it for another day as you never know when you may need to be apart from your little one. It's a safety net to have that little milk-bank, but it is certainly not essential. There are two truths to know about expressing breast milk: firstly, not all 'good' breastfeeders are good expressers. Boobs might be more than capable of feeding a baby, but when it comes to filling a bottle with a pump they don't produce much. I know many women who can't produce more than 50 ml when pumping but easily feed a baby for months. The second truth is there is no such thing as the perfect pump. While people will evangelise about the electric pump versus the hand pump, you really don't know until you have a go, as it is so individual. Many of my patients find they don't need this expensive kit at all, and simply hand express. Once again, you have to discover what is right for you. And yes, you will feel like a dairy cow.

How do I know my baby is getting enough milk?

The answer is simple: you will just know. I can assure you of that. Whether you are breast-, bottle- or mixed-feeding the clear signs will be there, and you need to learn to look for them and have confidence in yourself to get this right. That's what you're designed for – meeting your baby's needs – and that is what you will be able to do. Even after four or five days into motherhood you will have learnt the signs that your baby has got a full tummy and is contented; you probably don't even realise you know that. Trust me, you know. You are the woman with the super-powers who knows these things. Within days of motherhood, you will be a feeding expert. A real one.

Imagine a bloke who's not eaten enough: grumpy, restless, attention-seeking, food-seeking and often seen screaming. This is exactly what babies are like when they're not fed enough. Like father, like son. We're all human, and your baby will behave exactly as you'd expect if he's hungry. Some basic clues a baby is feeding well:

1. He gets bigger. You can see this and feel this. You're holding him all the time, and you'll soon notice the change.

2. Wet, soggy nappies – good feeding means your baby is well hydrated and will be making wet nappies 6–8 times a day.

3. Pooing: nice healthy poos (see Chapter 7).

4. He'll be relaxed/contented/a bit 'drunk' after a feed.

5. He can wait a good 2–3 hours before the next feed. Obviously this naturally spaces out even further after the first few weeks.

6. The boob is empty – you will get to know pretty quickly the difference between a full boob, and a soft floppy empty one.

7. The bottle is empty – I don't need to explain that.

Some basic clues your baby is not feeding well:

1. He's not getting noticeably chubbier or rounder in the face.

2. You can't feel a distinct boob difference before he's fed and after.

3. He doesn't seem relaxed and contented after feeding.

4. He can't wait 2–3 hours for the next feed.

5. He doesn't produce regular, soggy nappies.

6. He does dry, dark poos.

7. He seems generally irritable.

If instinct or any of the above signs tell you your baby may not be getting enough milk, see your midwife, health visitor or GP *quickly*. This is not a time to wait. Feeding babies also involves hydrating them, and they get dehydrated very quickly. If you think your baby is under-feeding, see your GP or midwife the same day. This is even worth an A&E trip if you can't get hold of anyone.

Weighing your baby

I don't really come across many second- or third-time mummies who weigh their babies regularly. Likewise, all of my doctor friends gave up weighing their babies after the six-week check. It is really not essential. Unless you have been advised otherwise by a healthcare professional, there is no need to have regular weighing trips, and certainly no need for baby scales at home.

Of course it's important to know that your baby is getting bigger but you are the best judge of that. Along with Daddy and the proud grandparents, you know best, and you don't need a figure on the scales to confirm it. Second-time mums, like doctors, have the confidence in their own ability to judge, and you should too. You just need to learn to trust yourself in the same way: be guided by your instinct and the baby. If you think your baby's thighs are getting chunkier, then they are!

By 10 days old, a baby should have regained his birthweight and the midwife coming to the house will check that before discharging you. This is important and a good sign for you to have confidence and carry on. At the six-week check you'll have another weigh-in, and to be honest you don't need any more. If you feel your baby is going in the right direction, there is no need to weigh him regularly.

If you have been advised to weigh your baby because there is a concern about poor weight gain, then of course it is essential you follow that advice. If not, just watch his cheeks getting chubbier and have the confidence that that is enough. You are the expert: listen to yourself.

But surely there's no harm in weighing a baby weekly or fortnightly, right? Well actually, aside from the fact it's an inconvenience in your otherwise hectic schedule, I think there can be, to be honest ... for two reasons.

Firstly, as a mum I want you to learn to trust yourself and be guided by your own intuition and instinct. If you are always reliant on the scales and the figures they tell you then it undermines mummy-power. Mummy-power must not be diluted! You know best. You don't need scales to tell you that you're doing a good job: you just need to squidge your baby's thighs, or notice his newborn vests are getting tight. It doesn't need to be more scientific than that. If you are concerned you can't feel your baby getting bigger, of course at that stage it's important to weigh him. But if you're comfortable those fat bracelets are getting fatter, there's really no need to bother.

Secondly, weighing just for the sake of weighing can lead to unnecessary anxiety, which I see time and time again in clinic. It is not unusual for a mummy to bring her baby to see me because 'The health visitor told me the baby was fat'. This craziness is a result of those centile charts where a baby's weight is plotted. Well, if you try to objectively measure a baby's fatness just on weight and a centile reading, pretty much all will come out too fat or too thin. Centile charts are far too standardised: every mum gets the same red health record book in this country – how can the same chart be used for all male babies when they start off different sizes, different ethnic origins, with different genes and different feeding? It doesn't make any sense. Sure, a centile chart is useful when there's been a problem but weighing your baby, when you're not worried about him in the first place, leads to false problems. Like being told he's too fat when he's not. And that causes unnecessary anxiety, guilt and feelings of failure that are to be entirely avoided.

- Keep calm
- Trust yourself
- You are your baby's feeding expert

Wind – and what to do

There ain't nothing more satisfying than hearing a ginormous burp come from your baby. While passing wind from either end is generally frowned upon in most Western societies, babies are totally exempt from this rule. In fact, you will notice yourself positively beaming with pride when your little one happily erupts. Grandmothers will clap, fathers will boast to Facebook and the world will cheer when your baby burps. Well, as I've learnt from a decade in general practice: there's nowt as queer as folk and we just love hearing our babies burp.

There are no laws regarding winding and burping your baby. Whether breast- or bottle-feeding, babies take in air and it needs to come out. You will learn what works for your baby.

As a general guide, it makes sense to see if your baby takes a natural pause when feeding: this is often the case and is your cue to help him get that gas out. If he doesn't seem to take a natural pause, try winding him about half-way through a feed; if this makes him cry and fret because you've interrupted his lunch, it will make him take in more air and you'll be going round in burp-filled circles. So be guided by him. As long as he is comfortable after a feed, you've got the right wind action-plan! Learn what he wants and go with it.

Some babies have very little wind and need no help at all getting it out. You will learn your baby's gas habits very quickly. If your baby is settled after feeding with no grimacing and no bother, having not burped, then so be it. Lucky you! You have an efficient winder.

I'm not sure if there really is a good way to wind a baby or we've just devised methods to occupy ourselves while waiting for that burp to come. Perhaps if you just sit with baby and wait it would take the same length of time! The rubbing and patting may just be a pastime for mummies on burp-waiting duty.

I definitely had windy babies and always found myself sitting rubbing their backs after each feed. We sat, I patted, they grimaced, I patted, they grimaced some more, I patted, then they grimaced again. Eventually after what felt like four years, and my arm had gone to sleep, I would be rewarded with a resounding belch. Their dad on the other hand seemed to just be able to pick them up, give them some fatherly knowing look, and the burp would spontaneously appear in minutes. He claims he just had 'the knack'. I claim he just has that effect on people.

If you don't trust the 'just waiting' method and you need to help your baby get his wind out, there are some different approaches that you can try:

1. After feeding, rest your baby upright on your chest with his head resting on your shoulder. This stretches his body and his guts and theoretically helps the gas come out, while you gently rub his back. It also means the burp arrives in your ear so you can't miss that joyous moment. Bad luck if he possets (see below) at the same time.

2. Sitting your baby up is another popular way of burping, supporting his body with one hand and rubbing or patting his back with another. This can be a little tricky with a newborn as supporting the head and body often takes up all the hands you've got; but once your newborn has better head control, after about six weeks, it can be a good burp technique.

3. Some babies burp well if you put them on their tummy on your lap, and gently rub their back. However, putting pressure on their tummies can cause some vomiting so it doesn't work well for everyone.

Once you have a method that works for you and your baby, stick with it. There is no right or wrong way as long as your baby is contented after feeding. Think about yourself after a big Sunday roast: contented, a bit dozy and relaxed – this is exactly how your baby should be after a feed. If he has not let out the wind and is uncomfortable, he'll be squirmy, grimacing and unsettled. You will know because you are your baby's wind expert. Watch and learn from him.

Reflux – the difference between posset and vomit

It is normal, and pretty standard for babies to bring up a little milk after they have fed. This happens whether they are breast- or bottle-fed, and has the charming name, 'posseting'. I can't accurately quantify a normal amount of posset, but it is not really bigger than a tablespoon – sometimes a little more, sometimes a little less. It isn't anything that would make you think, 'Oooo, that was a lot of vomit.'

The important thing is that a posset is a happy vomit: no pain, no discomfort or crying; it normally comes out with a burp and maybe a grimace, and it tends to just dribble out rather than be anything violent or impressive. This is what muslins were invented for and why all mothers are decorated with that over-the-shoulder white streak down their clothes. All babies do this and it's perfectly normal in an otherwise contented baby.

On the other hand, some babies vomit a lot after most feeds and you do think to yourself, 'Wow, that was a lot of vomit.' If you often need to change clothes after feeding (yours and your baby's) because of the quantity of vomit, then an alarm bell should start to ring. Likewise if vomiting is distressing, your baby is uncomfortable after feeding, uncomfortable lying down or is arching his back, these are signs that something is not right with his feeding. This could be a condition called reflux, where milk travels back up from the stomach after feeding, and you should speak to your GP about it.

I see a lot of reflux in babies – doctors think as many as half of all babies could have it. If your little one is not comfortable with feeding, and showing any of these reflux signs, see your GP as soon as you can. Feeding should be pleasurable and comforting for your baby (just as it is for adults) so it's worth getting reflux sorted out sooner rather than later.

- Keep calm
- Trust your instinct
- Listen to the baby expert: YOU

Chapter 4
Crying – Your Baby's Way of Communicating

Crying is perfectly normal. That is what babies do. Like pooing, weeing, feeding and sleeping, it's part of the normality of a baby's life. Babies do most of their crying in the first two months after they're born and the chances are so will you. While your sensible-person brain knows that of course this is normal, it still gets pretty stressful at the start when you have absolutely no idea why your perfect baby is crying and what on earth you're supposed to be doing about it.

Well, do not panic. Your super-mummy skills will kick in very quickly and you'll be the expert in no time without having followed any rules. Learning to cope with your baby's crying is as much about learning to look after yourself as it is about looking after your baby. Trusting yourself and listening to that fabulous instinct is vital. Keeping calm is hard but you'll manage that too.

Unfortunately, despite the natural powers of evolution, our babies still have just one gruesome way of communicating disapproval with us: crying, screaming, bawling, howling. I suppose if it sounded like a mild whimper, it wouldn't have the desired effect on us parents to REACT! So while it sounds awful and desperate, most of the time your baby is complaining about nothing more serious than having a dirty botty or wanting an extra ounce of milk, and you are more than capable of sorting her out.

Crying is not a reflection of your parenting skills. Babies cry in the same way as adults talk. It's just their way of telling us grown-ups how it is. It sounds dreadful but it usually is for no big deal. Coping and reacting to crying involves:

- Listening to your instinct (if you can hear it above all that crying).
- Keeping calm (yes, I know it's not easy).
- Taking control.
- Trusting your judgement.
- Understanding crying is merely a way of communication, not a sign of failure.

Learning your baby's cries

I won't patronise you by writing a list of reasons why your baby cries because it is perfectly obvious. You as a parenting expert will learn this. If there is an answer as to why your baby is crying, you'll find it by looking at her, not by reading this book.

Quite frankly, the list could be endless anyway, ranging from 'because your boob is empty and I'm having a growth spurt' to 'because my left foot is itchy'. You will learn all of these and you certainly don't need to be taught them. This is where that all-knowing instinct shines through and you have to keep calm and trust yourself. Even after a few weeks of being a super-mamma, you'll get it. Not because anyone has told you, but because you've found out yourself.

It is laughable for me to tell you that your baby cries when she is hungry or overtired. Babies cry for a whole host of reasons, many of which simply fall into the category – 'just because I want to'. Accepting this is a vital part of enjoying parenthood.

Not all babies cry for the same reasons. I had one baby who was perfectly happy to sit in poop, while the other needed a pristine derriere at all times. One of my patients is certain her baby cries when he has a wet nappy – this is not the norm, especially given today's super-duper dry nappies. But she changes him and he settles, as simple as that. It doesn't really matter if it isn't what babies are 'supposed' to do. It's what her baby does, and listening to her instinct rather than anything else gave her the solution. Her mum told her it means he'll be easy to potty-train. I have no idea what it means, but it beautifully illustrates that all babies are different: they don't follow the instruction manual, because there is no instruction manual.

You'll learn to understand your baby's cries without even trying. Not because you have memorised the tones, but because you will know the times of day she's tired or hungry and recognise the signs to match. This will happen naturally over the first few weeks without any guidelines or criteria. You don't need to sit down and try to learn this. Your baby will have her unique code for you, her own idiosyncrasies that make her bawl, and within a few weeks you'll be a super-expert extraordinaire in the crying game.

There are some schools of thought that believe you can tell what is the matter with babies by the type of cry they make. Perhaps this is true. I'm more inclined to believe you know why your baby is crying because you are her mother and you just 'know'. I have babies crying at me every week in clinic, and I couldn't tell you the difference between the cries because I'm not their mummy.

There is a different cry when your baby is ill (see Chapter 9), but you will also notice other things that will alert you something is wrong and it's this 'bigger picture' that you must always look at. Poor feeding, different poos, tiredness and other factors, as well as a cry that sounds more high-pitched and desperate.

As babies get older they will start to cry for different reasons: frustration at toys, you leaving the room, horrible-tasting vegetables and a million other things you will know and won't need to be taught.

There isn't always an answer

One of the most important lessons to teach yourself as a mum is that there isn't always an answer to why your baby is crying. Some babies cry more than others. Some days your baby will cry more than other days. Babies are not predictable automatons (thankfully, otherwise life would be *very* boring) and there will be times when you just don't know what the bloomin' 'eck is going on. Even though my children are now fully versed in the English language, I still sometimes don't know why they are upset. Accept it. That is okay.

This is not me saying, 'Leave her to cry, ignore her and go out for a pint.' This is me saying, 'Look after her, soothe her but don't drive yourself potty looking for what may be an elusive answer.' As long as your baby is safe and fed and you're confident she's not unwell, then that's all right. You can't always have the answer to why she is crying. And that is okay. You will not find the answer in an encyclopaedic list and you have to acknowledge that only your baby has the answer. But you can still be in control!

There isn't always an answer to lots of things parents want to know. Why do some babies get more colds than others? There isn't an answer. Why do some babies walk at one year, some not until they're two? There isn't always an answer. We're all on a spectrum. It's not one-size-fits-all.

Of course you will try to deal with the most obvious causes of crying and ensure your baby is not unwell, but beyond that you may just have to accept she is having a bad day. And so are you. Keep calm and go with it. It is perfectly fine to say, 'I have no idea why my baby is crying, but I know she is fine.' That doesn't make you a failed parent, it makes you a brilliantly sensible expert.

Imagine if this baby was actually your fourth baby, chances are you wouldn't have time to try to establish the exact cause of her crying each time because you'd be busy on the school run. So as long as she was safe, secure and well you'd happily say, 'I don't know.' Sometimes you need to go with that thought, otherwise you can drive yourself a bit bananas.

Having a baby who seems to relish a good howl makes you a perfect target for competitive mum banter:

- 'Oh, I hardly hear a peep out of Toby.'
- 'Goodness, she cries a lot doesn't she?'
- 'Maybe you're doing something wrong.'

Well, you're not doing anything wrong at all. The amount your precious little thing cries, bawls, howls is not a reflection of your parenting skills. Never let other people make you feel in the slightest bit inadequate or guilty through their dim-witted remarks. Competitive comments speak volumes about the people making them and their own shortcomings, not yours. Never give rhetoric like this a second thought. (See Chapter 8 for more on competitive mums.)

Crying in public

There will be times when it just won't be terribly convenient that your baby is screaming her head off. You will try everything and still she will scream. It's just the start of a long list of ways she will develop to embarrass you. All babies cry. All babies scream. Your baby won't know what's a good time to get going with a good bawl, but you'll see she'll manage with perfect precision to choose the worst time. This clearly proves she is a genius.

Every single member of the mummy-club endures this delightful treat of parenting: I can promise you, it's not just you who is so blessed. Such fond memories I have of my darlings screaming on aeroplanes, in restaurants, in the library ... they really are champions at choosing the worst times.

People just *love* interfering when your baby is crying. I don't know why folk stare or tut at babies crying on the bus. It is very annoying as all babies have these moments – the trouble is you feel like a bit of a freak when it happens to you. Well, believe me, it's the people who are tutting at a crying baby who are weirdoes, not you.

Ignore. Ignore. Ignore. Unless someone is offering to hold the baby for you or buy you some chocolate, just ignore them. This is fantastic practice for when the very same people are staring at you when your darling becomes a toddler and starts having fully blown tantrums on buses. Never ever get involved with someone expressing disdain at your crying baby. Just pretend you can't speak their language and ignore them.

Could my baby be ill?

If you feel your baby cries just too much or too often, even for *you*, or there is something not right, you should always chat this through with an understanding GP. A good doctor would never send you away or make you feel stupid for seeking advice if you are concerned about your baby.

The worst that can happen is that you will be reassured that your baby is fine and you have nothing to worry about. It doesn't make you a failing mother because you asked the GP about her crying, it makes you a great mother because you followed your instinct. You should not feel guilty about this, you should feel empowered and in control for doing the right thing.

What should I use to soothe her?

How you choose to comfort your baby beyond the kisses and cuddles is entirely up to you. There is no right or wrong. No rules to follow (hurray) and little scope to get this 'wrong'. These kind of things tend to just happen by happy unplanned accident, as opposed to being chosen. There might be experts telling you their comforter is 'right', but the only 'right' one is the one that works for your little one.

The ideal comforter has to be convenient and readily available whether you're at home or on the move. So, for example, if her comforter is always a boob, then that's pretty inconvenient when you're on a spa weekend with the girls and baby is at home with her dad. If you have no plans to ever be away from her for the first years and you want your boob to be her comfort, then it will work well for you and that is the right comforter for you and her.

A comforter also has to be replaceable and easy to find. Muslins always worked well in our house because they were readily available. I could buy them cheaply in packs of 20 and they were pretty easy to find and replace. Replaceability is a massive issue with comforters: my niece who grew up in New York always had the same Sesame Street Elmo as a comforter: she fell asleep with him from early on and he was her soother. Yes, very cute you might think. It was, until of course she lost the one and only Elmo. My brother-in-law resorted to putting 'LOST' posters all over Manhattan, but Elmo was never recovered much to everyone's dismay. So have a little think if you're going to let baby be comforted by a one-off teddy. Make sure the one-off teddy has a couple of doppelgangers hidden away in a cupboard for emergencies. Try to encourage the use of replaceable and available soothers: this is why muslins, blankies and thumbs have been used for centuries – because savvy mums realise they're convenient for parents, never mind their babies!

In the early days many different things will comfort your baby and gradually she'll find her favourite. It will just evolve naturally, but you can put something next to her whenever she sleeps or give her the same thing whenever she cries. I have come across weird and wonderful ways to comfort babies both in my clinic and at home. Up until my son was aged two he was comforted by a muslin both when he was upset and when he was tired. It had worked well by happy accident for his older sister, so I encouraged him to have one as well. Pretty normal, right? Yes, except he didn't hold it or just rub it on his face like textbook babies do: he used to stick the corner of the muslin right in the corner of his eye. Much as I adore the kid, even I have to admit that is pretty eccentric.

I can't possibly fathom why on earth he found this reassuring, I assume it's a weirdness from his father's side of the family, but it worked for him. And he seems highly normal in all other ways. He hasn't gone on to stick other things in his eye.

I've had more than one baby arrive in my GP clinic with a bra lying next to them in their pram. The first time I saw this, I thought Mum had had a massive wardrobe malfunction in the waiting room. But actually not. Newborn babies like to feel and sense their mummies for comfort, and new mums often try this bra thing in the early days – if your baby can smell you or the milk, she may settle. Shove a bra in the cot and your baby thinks you're close by: well, it's nicer than a pair of your socks I suppose. Whatever works; as long as you're laid back about who gets to see your underwear.

So what about that hotbed of parenting debate: the dummy? Dummies have evolved from being common to being *common*. Once highly disapproved of, dummies are now a very widespread way to soothe babies. As with many aspects of parenting, it is an issue parents-to-be have strong opinions on which changes quite radically when the baby actually arrives. It is incredibly easy to have an opinion on dummies before you have been faced with an angry baby screaming blue murder at 3am and everything else has failed. That is why it is so normal for me to hear a new mum say, 'I wasn't going to use a dummy, but …'. You don't really know how easy or hard you're going to find settling your baby, and a dummy might be the answer YOU find.

It is not wrong or right to use a dummy. Dummies have been used for centuries to pacify babies because they work. In the first few weeks, babies have a very strong sucking reflex and get comforted both emotionally and physically by the action of sucking, which also helps to relieve wind and can soothe tummies.

Using a dummy is not something to feel guilty about and it does not mean you have failed because you found no other way to soothe your baby. Some babies take to dummies, while others don't use them at all. Often this is not down to anything mums have done, but simply a baby's preference. I have had plenty of frazzled mums say to me they wished their babies *would* use a dummy as it seems like a convenient, handy way to settle a baby but their babies were not interested in them.

In reality, the time you decide to use a dummy will not be a zen, chilled situation where you can weigh up the pros and cons of the decision. It is more likely you will be in a state of panic about your crying baby and you will be screaming at anyone to run down to Boots to get you one. And that is absolutely fine: necessity is after all the mother of invention.

When you get into a slightly calmer state (and I promise you will) have a little think about the 'dummy debate' just so you can make the right decision for you and your little one. I don't care whether people disapprove about you using a dummy: many a woman at a bus stop will give you an opinion on dummy-use. The best one I have heard is that it is associated with a later age of walking: clearly that falls into the category of absolutely absurd nonsense. But you need to be aware of why *real* experts have some concerns about dummies.

Mum-experts I know have often regretted using a dummy overnight, when they realise it's they who have to get up every so often to find it in the cot. Until baby can find it himself, it will most likely be you on the dummy-hunt, so you need to be prepared for that.

Prolonged sucking of anything whether it is a dummy or a thumb can eventually cause problems with teeth development and the way your baby's mouth develops. This is actual science and dentists know that this can cause a problem. There is certainly real concern about kids who are using dummies beyond toddlerhood into their third or fourth years.

One of the few rules that makes oodles of sense is to use an orthodontic dummy. Dentists (i.e. experts in this area) believe an orthodontic dummy is less likely to cause mouth problems so it is a guideline worth heeding. Using a dummy early on before six months is unlikely to have these physical effects, *but* at this time your baby is developing a habit. So be a bit clever with the dummy: start to wean your baby off the dummy even before she knows she loves it. Once you're through the first few months of craziness, and you've honed your super-mum extraordinaire skills and are feeling less zombified, your baby will probably need a dummy less so follow her lead and use it less.

Try to keep it just for home, just for naps or just for bedtime. Things do evolve and change as your baby gets older. She'll cry less, so when you notice her wanting the dummy less, empower that and use it less. Don't assume just because you've started with a dummy, she'll always need one to calm down. As she's older and more alert, other things may calm her when she's angry or upset: like a cuddle and a tickle from you. Watch for that, and you'll find your own little pathway to using it less.

Don't always have a dummy in your changing bag: then both of you will have to find other ways to cope while you're out, and you will from very early on. Make sure YOU are not solely reliant on the dummy to comfort your baby and she'll follow suit.

Dummies are for settling and soothing. They are not meant as a plug or for face decoration. Using them with caution will make it a very easy habit to break and there won't be any danger of reducing all that gorgeous babbling your baby is going to do.

When mums in the clinic ask me if I approve of dummies I advise to use one if it works for you, but to always have a plan in the back of your mind of how you're going to get rid of it. At some point you will have to wean her off a dummy. Now that isn't a reason not to use one, but it is a reason to be savvy about using one.

And yes, dummies do need sterilising. As long as you are sterilising bottles and other things that go into your baby's mouth, you should be sterilising dummies.

- Listen to yourself
- Keep calm
- If it works for your baby, then it's right

Colic – and how to manage it

There is really only one important thing to know about colic: it just gets better.

Colic by definition is unexplained crying for three hours a day, on at least three days a week, in a baby under three months old. That is a hell of a lot of crying. Colic involves crying for no reason in an otherwise healthy, thriving baby who will be inconsolable no matter what you do. And often the crying is in the latter part of the day – just when you are completely frazzled and would also like to scream for two hours. This is what makes it so stressful.

Despite all our scientific knowledge these days, no one actually knows what causes colic. When you don't understand the problem, finding the solution is pretty damn tricky so you're starting on the back foot.

There are a lot of theories about why babies get colic – some scientific, some codswallop. For many people there is an assumption that it's all down to your baby's guts. Colic is actually not always linked to tummy trouble. For most babies I have examined with true colic, there is no answer to why they have it. They feed beautifully, grow well, poop normally and are happy bunnies in the day. But in the evening they cry inconsolably for hours and that is very hard to deal with.

Fraught parents understandably try many things out of desperation with colic. But I have to be brutally honest: please, please, please don't waste lots of time and effort searching for a solution to colic because I'm afraid for most babies there isn't one. And you can drive yourself into a frenzy of guilt, madness and failure trying to search for that elusive answer. Coping with colic is one thing. Coping with the failure and guilt of not being able to solve it is a whole different ball game. So protect yourself from that by accepting the reality of colic.

The honest answer to handling colic is learning to manage the crying, rather than finding an expensive solution that doesn't exist. There is definitely not a one-size-fits-all answer to colic: soothing, holding and patience are your best bet.

When parents are desperate to find a solution for colic, I see mums spending a lot of money trying a load of potential solutions, often all at once. And the truth is 'something' normally works around the time the baby is three months old, which is when she has grown out of it naturally.

People try colic/lactase drops, gripe water, forms of massage and cranial osteopathy, teas, homeopathy, special bottles. I even met someone who tried special music for her baby (it didn't work). For every mum I meet who finds colic drops helpful, I see another mum who finds them useless. The same goes for gripe water and every other magic colic tonic. You will hear compelling stories from people whose babies cried non-stop until that miraculous day they took him to the cranial osteopath at three months and the bawling stopped. Unfortunately, this is an expensive placebo. The crying was going to stop at three months anyway.

If an expert or product promises you they have a

guaranteed answer to colic, they don't. Cynicism and instinct is important here, which is very difficult in the face of exhaustion and evenings of screaming ahead. It's important to protect yourself from the false hope of these remedies, which can lead to terrible disappointment. That's not to say the vaguely scientific ones aren't worth trying: they are – just be savvy as to what miracles you can expect. An honest action plan for colic:

1. Have a chat with a doctor to confirm it is 'simply' colic.
2. Try maybe one or two easy, non-expensive solutions at different times.
3. Work out an action plan to deal with the crying.
4. Put your baby's three-month birthday in your diary, and look forward to that date.

Of course you will want to try at least one colic solution and that is what every sensible mum would do. I would gently suggest you try those things that are easy and cheap like the special feeding bottles, increasing evening feeding or giving colic drops. Desperate for a solution you might be tempted to throw in all the ammunition at once. Don't, because you have to do your own scientific experiment. If you try everything all at once, you will have no idea what works.

Do not ignore other symptoms. Colic can be mistaken for reflux (see page 57), lactose intolerance or other tummy trouble so look out for other signs. If your baby is unsettled all day after feeding, or she's not gaining weight well, or her poo is a bit odd (see Chapter 7), there's more to this than colic. Colic doesn't always need to be diagnosed by a doctor, but actually the reassurance of knowing it is colic can very much help you to get by.

It takes a lot of resilience to deal with non-stop crying and there will be many evenings when you too are in tears. Try to formulate your own personal action plan for dealing with the crying. This could include:

- Taking it in shifts. It doesn't always have to be you holding the baby. It could be Granny, Dad, a friend or your neighbour – anyone will do.
- Putting your baby down for a few minutes safely in her cot. Take a few deep breaths and go back in to get her.
- Using a baby sling to hold and comfort her. At least then your hands are free to text a friend for support.
- Accepting she has colic and that is not your fault.
- Reassuring yourself it is a phase and it will get better.
- Asking for help if it gets too much: never ever feel afraid to do this.

The reality of life with a baby with colic is it is very draining and very upsetting. It is testing to relationships and makes you feel pretty awful in the early days of motherhood. Every mum with a colicky baby feels like this: remember it just gets better. Time and patience are your friend. Trust yourself to get through it and listen to yourself. You are the super-mummy expert and you will find your own way to get through the hard times. In a few months, these screamy and stressful evenings will seem like a distant memory.

- Keep calm
- Trust your instinct
- Listen to the baby expert: YOU

Chapter 5
How Are You Feeling? The Highs and the Lows

Now that you've given birth, not many people are going to be particularly interested in how you feel. I'm sorry if that sounds callous; it's simply reality. It's not that nobody cares about you any more, it's simply that your 9 lb red-faced bundle (who does absolutely nothing apart from feed and poo) is right now far more fascinating than you. Even your own mum will phone and not ask how you are, she'll just ask about the baby. From now on all anyone will actually ever talk to you about is THE BABY.

So while the whole world is talking about your baby and the smell of his latest nappy contents, wouldn't it be nice to have a chance to think about how YOU are feeling in your new life?

Once you give birth who you are changes massively – for most women this is the biggest transformation that will ever happen, more so than any other life event. It's like the most momentous makeover of your life, and then some. So it shouldn't come as any surprise that you may not be feeling as 'normal' as you were before. Except it does come as a big surprise, right?

The evolution into parenthood isn't simply a role change: it is a physical, mental, social, emotional and, for most of us, an all-consuming transformation. This isn't about saggy boobs and silvery stretch marks, although those are of course a big part of this transformation. This change for you is about *everything*: every single aspect of your existence changes, from the minutiae of day-to-day life to your aspirations and dreams. Even your position in society alters. People see you differently, you see yourself differently and you are treated differently. You are now A MOTHER. So, of course, you feel different. I still don't know if I even feel grown-up enough to be 'a mother', and I've been doing it for 10 years.

I've noticed mums and dads who I meet in my clinic are generally unprepared for this big shift in reality. I certainly had no idea how enormous this change was going to be, and I know from the women I look after that few are ready for it. When I ask new parents how they're finding new motherhood, the majority of mums simply say, 'It's very different.'

Antenatal classes are geared up to prepare you for birth, but are very bad at preparing for anything after that! You will have been fed a lot of information about the practical and physical aspects of caring for a baby, for example what paraphernalia you need to buy, but very little about the emotional changes in you. So while you may be 100 per cent up-to-speed on which breast-pad is best, you've not really contemplated that you might be crying every day for two weeks.

The trouble with this lack of preparation is that motherhood can feel like a big shock to the system (as if having what feels like an 8-tonne torpedo pass through your perineum isn't shock enough). And chances are you'll end up feeling like you are the only woman crying at the nappy adverts. Well, let me tell you sister, you're not. Most mums feel completely strange while they get used to parenthood.

It also doesn't help that new mummies are tricked – us women are fed a little lie that baby pops out, you sling him into the papoose, and carry on where you left off. Photos of stunning celebs with gorgeous mini-mes sitting on their hip like the latest fashion accessory trick us into thinking life is the same, just with babe in tow. Well, I'm sorry to break the news to you, but that ain't real life. In reality, for your average new mum (that's you!) that's miles away from where you're at right now. Learn to have a bit of a giggle at those celeb mamma photos, otherwise you'll start to feel incredibly and unnecessarily inadequate!

Motherhood is fabulous but your emotions can be sent on a scary-as-hell roller coaster for a few months, or years. So let's take a moment to think about how YOU are feeling right now.

Craziness of life in the first few weeks

In many cultures around the world, for example in India, after having a baby the women adopt a period of rest for as many as 40 days, during which time they rest and are pampered: they call this *postnatal confinement*. They are not supposed to do any physical work, and they are allowed to recuperate and simply look after their baby. This gives them a chance to physically and mentally recover from pregnancy and labour. In my opinion, this is such a fabulous idea that I'm trying to adopt it as an annual event in my house without the pregnancy, birth, baby or breastfeeding bits.

On the flipside, in the UK, us mums try to push ourselves far too hard after birth: this starts the moment that placenta is delivered when we're kicked out of hospital, often before the epidural has had a chance to wear off, and sent on our way. We expect to be back in the shops, back in the gym, even back in the sack not so much as a fortnight later. But the truth is you just need to calm down and chill.

I have ladies who come and see me within three weeks of giving birth worried they don't feel like themselves and worrying they can't manage to juggle the baby and 'normal' things. 'Normal' things seem to include shopping, coffee, making dinner, waxing ...

A mum who once came to see me, worried about her episiotomy stitches, apologised because she hadn't shaved her legs: her baby was only 10 days old.

Newsflash *You don't need to achieve anything in the first eight weeks after having your baby.*

The thing is, after having your first baby – there is no 'normal'. The reason for this is that there is actually no time for normality. Feeding, changing, washing muslins and generally cooing over your baby takes 25 hours a day and there is little room for anything else. Plus, you also need time to nap if you are going to recover well from your pregnancy and birth. So if you are pressurising yourself on top of that to make plans or worry about underarm depilation, you are pushing yourself far too much.

- Keep everything calm so you stay calm
- Listen to your body
- Trust yourself to know how much is 'too much'

Every single mum experiences this craziness after giving birth. It is not just you. It's vital to remember this as you can be fooled into thinking it's only *your* baby that takes every waking second of the day to look after. It certainly isn't. This is very normal and is absolutely nothing to worry or feel guilty about.

I admit, it is quite surprising just how much time looking after a newborn takes but that's how it is, and you'll enjoy yourself and him far more if you accept it. And when you see a photo of a celeb who's just given birth, remember she has staff, a great deal of airbrushing and she is probably still feeling shattered. Remember, you're supposed to be laughing at those pics.

I tell all the mummies I look after, if you've brushed your teeth by the time you go back to bed at the end of the day, you've already done very well and should be proud. If you've had a chance to wash your hair, you're an overachiever in my opinion. In the first month or two, there is really little time for anything else as your bundle of joy will have used up every moment. And you're also damned tired.

Your postnatal period is a time to embrace tracksuit bottoms, daytime TV, your sofa and online grocery shopping. This is why you spent the last few months of your pregnancy 'nesting' – so you can enjoy and relax in your nest. In the first eight weeks, you don't need to be doing anything else.

Crucially, when you are sleep deprived and recovering from labour, it is not worth wasting what vital precious energy you have on anything other than yourself or your baby. Visitors can make their own tea, and yours for that matter. Daddies can make their own dinner and discover some previously hidden laundry skills. And the iron can stay in the cupboard ad infinitum. (Mine remains there a decade later.)

Seriously, the first few weeks are about prioritising what needs to be done and pretty much ignoring everything else. This is the recipe for keeping calm. There are no rules about what you should be doing, you just need to protect yourself from over-doing it.

Coping with the craziness of the first few weeks involves developing these vital skills for new motherhood:

- Saying yes to all offers of help – some of us aren't very good at accepting help. We think we should be coping all by ourselves. That's fine in theory but if someone says 'let me hold the baby while you have a shower/snooze/sandwich/browse on Facebook' the answer is always YES.

- Embrace online shopping in all forms – there is a reason the internet was invented. Lugging a newborn baby round Sainsbury's is not fun. Having everything delivered to the house is.
- Be discerning with your guest list – only guests bringing food or happiness should be allowed in.
- You must have no guilt regarding what you should be doing. Ignore thoughts along the lines of 'I'm a terrible wife/daughter/friend as I only have time to look after the baby'. You should be doing NOTHING other than looking after a baby.

Advice versus instinct – prepare for battle!

In case you weren't feeling befuddled enough having just given birth, there's a whole army of people out there trying to make you feel even more mad. I bet you have already met one or two …

The whole impetus for writing this book was the fact that every mum I have ever met, whether friend, relative, patient, or random woman at a bus stop, complained about the crazy, conflicting, confusing advice she was bombarded with as a new mum. I'd like to promise it will be different for you, but it won't. Forewarned is forearmed so prepare yourself for battle!

The sheer quantity of advice on offer when you become parents is immense and the majority of it is useless, unnec-essary and serves only to undermine your own fabulous maternal instinct. The official and written guidelines are one thing and even that is often too much (see Chapter 11 on weaning!) But then there is the face-to-face advice people offer: and it will take your utmost strength and calm not to feel frazzled and bewildered by this.

Every single person you have ever met, plus everyone else, will offer some advice or an opinion about your newborn. The majority of this advice is unwarranted. A vast amount is wrong. Some is downright dangerous. But everyone has got something to say about your baby, what you should be doing with him and, without exception, why they are right.

You will have noticed this advising, or *meddling* as I prefer to call it, started when you were pregnant:

- 'Goodness, you're big for six months' – a favourite meddler comment usually said to a perfectly normal-sized pregnant woman.
- 'You're carrying all at the front; it must be a boy' – said to me when I was pregnant with my daughter.
- 'You're carrying so high; it must be a girl' – said to me when I was pregnant with my son.
- 'Oh, it's fine to eat raw eggs when you're pregnant. I'm sure that's just doctors being over-cautious' – errr, no it's not.

This meddling is not such a problem when you are pregnant. Everyone is excited, they're trying to be friendly, it doesn't really matter. But once your baby is born the game changes. You do actually need the advice, often you've been desperately seeking some sensible help, usually about feeding or sleeping I find, and the trouble is it can be very hard to find decent consistent advice.

Time and time again frazzled new parents come into my clinic with stories of conflicting advice given to them by a whole host of people, professionals and online forums. And I have to make an apology as a healthcare professional that we are also guilty of giving conflicting advice and bewildering new parents rather than helping. New parents can go to their midwife, health visitor and GP and come away with completely different advice that ends up just bewildering rather than helping them. There is very little consistency in the advice given, which makes it very difficult to trust anyone. At this point you must:

- Trust yourself
- Remember you are the only expert your baby needs
- Keep calm in the face of perplexing advice

A new daddy said to me once in clinic he couldn't believe all the conflicting advice they were given when his wife needed help to establish breastfeeding. Within one 24-hour stretch in hospital, they'd had four different opposing opinions about how his wife should be breastfeeding the baby:

1. One midwife thought she was doing amazingly and had a 'perfect latch'.

2. Another said she was leaving the baby on far too long.

3. A third said there was no way she would be able to feed without nipple shields.

4. Six hours later the fourth person likened nipple shields to the devil explaining she's now ruined her chances of breastfeeding forever (she went on to breastfeed for a year).

The experience was mystifying and upsetting, but a great early lesson for them as parents.

'Whose advice do you take now?' I asked tentatively.

'I Skype my mum in Canada, and we ignore everyone else!' he replied.

This is certainly not an unusual story for me to hear. Which begs the question, why does this end up happening? The simple answer is often there is no scientifically proven right or wrong way of doing things. People are giving you their advice based on their own experience and this may not be right for you. Plus people can get very dogmatic in their approach to matters such as how to feed a baby and how to put on a babygro, often feeling compelled to give you their advice in a very dictatorial style. I once had a random encounter in a supermarket when another woman in the queue tried to tell me why I shouldn't be using a baby sling. She was ranting as if I was giving my baby son a cigarette. I packed my shopping and whizzed off. I didn't wait for the explanation; chances are there wasn't one.

As I may have mentioned, just once or twice, there are genuinely important guidelines for a handful of things and the rest is simply opinion. Except the way it is often presented is as a religion! So you feel compelled to follow it, until two days later another expert gives you a different approach. The result is one confused, upset mummy. A formula I have seen time and time again in clinic.

From day one you have to trust your own maternal instinct. Start listening to your own opinions and learn to ignore the women in supermarket queues. You may not have been a mum for long, but you know what you are doing. Listening to yourself takes priority over listening to people dying to interfere. Your little one has all the expert he needs in you. Luckily even when your baby is but a few hours old, maternal instinct is all-powerful and I believe right.

I'm not saying don't listen to *any* advice. What I'm saying is always listen to your instinct at the same time to separate the wheat from the chaff. When everyone is giving you advice, and you're feeling frazzled, that instinct can get pushed aside and watered down by well-meaning pseudo-experts. But you mustn't let it. Just be selective with your hearing and readiness to take on board what meddlers are saying.

I know that the bombardment of real guidelines, pseudo-guidelines, meddlers and supposedly professional advice new mums now face can undermine your mummy-power. Don't let it! You are officially your baby's parenting guru: he doesn't need anything else. Lucky for him you are a super-mamma and you'll know what's right and what's wrong.

It is hard to know who to trust for good advice when you're a first-time mum, even among healthcare professionals; I *am* a healthcare professional and it was hard for me even to know.

Some words of warning:

- Never trust anyone who says *only* their way of parenting is right.
- If the advice feels wrong, chances are it probably is.
- If guidelines are sensible they will have been endorsed by the Royal College of Paediatrics, the World Health Organisation, the Royal College of Midwives, the Department of Health or a similar bona fide medical institution.
- To avoid confusion and inconsistency, try to choose one person to listen to, like my patient who learnt to phone his mum in Canada. My 'advisor' was the elderly health visitor I had whose mantra was 'Jolly good, well done'. She said this no matter what I told her I was doing with the baby. She instilled in me that my instinct was more important than anything.

I don't feel happy all the time

Feeling a bit down after giving birth is so common, it is pretty much normal. In the first 10 days, especially, your mood will feel all over the place because of the hormones flying around sorting out your milk, and making you feel crazy, tearful, super-happy, super-sad often all at the same time. This is a normal postnatal experience. You will find yourself crying at car insurance adverts on the telly. It's a bit weird, but completely stand-ard. My most impressively peculiar reaction was bawling my eyes out at a friend who offered to loan me her breast pump. I still don't know if I was crying from joy or misery; it was a pretty good pump.

Hormonal changes, exhaustion and the huge life-changing experience of BECOMING A PARENT, of course, are going to impact on your mood. It can be quite hard-hitting. This is not postnatal depression; this is what is termed baby blues and is fairly typical. I reckon most dads get it too after the birth of their first child, but few admit it.

You're expecting to feel like Mother Nature: all glow-ing and radiant with a polished halo and oodles of love and breast milk flowing from your body. Instead you're actually feeling rough mentally and you don't even want to mention what's flowing from your body because it's a bit grim.

It's a bit of a shock that you haven't turned into the Greek goddess of motherhood (yet) and you've worn the same pair of pyjamas since you got home from the hospital. Normal, normal, normal. This is an entirely normal part of the post-natal period. Whoop, whoop! Lucky you. But don't worry because for most women it passes after a couple of weeks.

Of course even after the first few weeks, there will be times when you have days of feeling low, are a bit weepy or generally fed up. Occasional days like this are completely standard for mums, just like they are for anyone else. These can be compounded by tiredness, a crying baby, cabin-fever and all the other woes and worries life throws at us. This is nothing to worry about or analyse: I would simply diagnose this as being human. Parenthood is magnificent but everyone has their bad days when it is impossible to keep calm. These days pass and you'll be back to feeling like that super-duper mamma in no time.

Becoming a parent often has a huge strain on your relationship and I've seen this come as quite a shock to parents. Exhaustion, hormones and the massive upheaval in both of your lives of course combines to create a strain on your relationship. Don't forget the first few weeks are hard for dads too as he's also tired and new to this parenting business. There's resentment on both sides: 'she's with the baby the whole time' or 'he's so lucky he can go back to work and his friends', and it can make for an unhappy time. This is so normal and commonplace. It takes time, patience from both of you and a degree of effort to sort yourselves out. This is yet another reason to do very little in the first few weeks: so if you do have the time, you can concentrate on the people that matter.

I also see and hear, many times, that mums don't always bond with their babies instantly. I think this is hard for mums to admit and it feels so ungrateful to verbalise it. We have massive expectations of motherhood when we are pregnant and the word 'bonding' really is overplayed: not everyone has that lightning bolt of love the moment they set eyes on their newborn. It can take time. And that is fine. It develops for many over days and weeks, not hours.

Boredom is another completely normal state of mind after you've given birth and while you are on maternity leave. Mothers don't think they're allowed to admit it, which is silly: just because life is great, and you love your baby, doesn't mean you can't feel a bit bored of the routine now and then. Feeling cheesed off, harking back to pre-baby times or wishing you were still at work, does not make you a bad mother. It makes you a perfectly normal woman in the 21st century. (Every woman in the 19th century would have thought this too, if they'd been allowed to.)

There is not one mum out there who has enjoyed every single moment of motherhood: of course you're allowed to feel bored. This is absolutely nothing at all to feel guilty about, and I promise you that everyone in your antenatal gang feels the same from time to time even if they don't admit it.

So baby blues, occasional bad days and boredom are all perfectly normal and natural. Everyone goes through this; I certainly did and it is not something that should concern you in the slightest. Keep calm about it and remind yourself it just makes you an ordinary mummy. You're one of us. Part of the gang.

What is not normal is postnatal depression. This is completely different from feeling low or bored or anxious because you don't really know what you're doing. When postnatal depression hits new mums, it strikes hard and you can't really mistake it. We think around 1 in 10 mums will experience postnatal depression – so while it's not the norm, it's certainly not uncommon.

The essential difference between feeling 'a bit down' and postnatal depression is that depression occurs on most days, and continues for a few weeks. There are very specific symptoms of depression and there is no obvious cause such as exhaustion or the baby being a bit difficult.

Time after time, mums say to me 'but I don't know why I'm depressed, I have a good baby, he's not difficult'. That's exactly the point – you can't rationalise postnatal depression. It hits people without warning: it has nothing to do with having a good baby, an easy baby or plenty of help. And possibly that makes it even harder, because you feel so guilty and unjustified in feeling sad. This can create a worsening vicious circle for your mood. But that is the hallmark of a true depression: there is no clear-cut reason for it, much the same as any other type of depression.

Clear signs of postnatal depression

If one or more of these symptoms occur on *most* days over a period of two weeks, you *could* be suffering with depression.

Not enjoying the good stuff, not being interested in yourself or your baby
Feeling weepy
Feeling guilty, unloved or that you are not a good mummy
Feeling as if you can't cope, even with the easy stuff
Lacking motivation to do anything for yourself or for the baby
Feeling irritated and irritable for no obvious reason
Feeling indecisive and unable to concentrate on or remember things
Feeling miserable

In conjunction with these symptoms mums with postnatal depression feel tired, have poor sleep and often feel less hungry. However, these symptoms are common in all other new mums too, so are not a great way to distinguish true depression. If at any point you recognise these symptoms in yourself, or instinctively you feel you may be suffering from postnatal depression, please, please, please seek help.

Mums can be scared to admit to postnatal depression for a catalogue of reasons that sadly can delay them getting the help they need. There are common myths about seeking help that need dispelling: these can be pretty dangerous as they can stop women getting the support they need. These are some of the reasons patients have told me they haven't sought help for their depression after giving birth:

- They're scared the baby could be taken away.
- They're scared it means they're not a good mother.
- They don't want to be addicted to anti-depressants.
- They're scared they won't bond with the baby.
- They're frightened people will judge them.
- They see it as an admission of weakness.

In reality:

- Babies are not taken away from the mother simply for having postnatal depression.
- Having postnatal depression does not mean you are a bad mother.
- Anti-depressants are not the only treatment and are not addictive.

- Mums with postnatal depression do bond with their babies.
- No one will judge you for having a medical problem.
- Postnatal depression is no more a sign of weakness than breaking your arm.

People are still not very good at talking about mental health problems. There is still an enormous and unnecessary stigma around psychological illnesses. A vast amount of my daily work as a GP is around the mental health of people – anyone can have a mental illness. It is certainly not a weakness, and in my mind seeking help for depression is no different from seeking help for diabetes.

If you think you may have the signs of postnatal depression, it is vital to get help at an early stage. There are two reasons for this: firstly, the sooner you start getting help, the easier it can be to treat before your mood plummets further and damaging thoughts and behaviours become your routine; secondly, sometimes accessing help can take time: if you are recommended a talking therapy the waiting list may be a few weeks so the quicker you're on that list, the better. No one with postnatal depression should ever be fobbed off as simply being a bit 'tired' or 'not coping' with new motherhood.

Once you're clear that your mood has some of the hallmarks of postnatal depression, first admit it to yourself, then tell your partner and go to see your GP together. Write down how you've been feeling before you go to the doctor: if this is the first time you've admitted to a healthcare professional about a mental health problem, it can be embarrassing and daunting. Having your symptoms ready to read out will ease the process. Do not feel embarrassed or ashamed; no GP should make you feel scared to admit these symptoms.

Going to the GP and admitting you possibly have post-natal depression does not mean an instant prescription for anti-depressants. I know a lot of people are afraid of this. Anti-depressants are a good treatment and for many women they can help and are necessary. This is something you will be involved in deciding with your GP. That is why I think it helps to take your partner along, because he can also help with some objective decision-making about the right treatment for YOU. Some women have counselling for this; some women have both types of treatment. Occasionally with mild postnatal depression, no treatment is needed at all, just reassurance and accept-ance can be enough.

This is still a time for that all-important instinct to shine. If tablets feel right to you and they've been suggested, then go for it. If you don't like the idea, for whatever reason, it is crucial to be honest with the doctor helping you. Likewise if you don't think you're a 'talking' kind of person, make sure you express this. Even if you are ill, you can still be empowered and listen to yourself. And any decision you make does not have to be conclusive; you can change your mind at any time if you start to feel worse or better.

However you may be feeling after you give birth and the months that follow, it is vital that you do not waste any time worrying about other people's opinions of you.

Your mental state, whether fantastic or shattered, is really no one else's business and the last thing you have time to think about is judgement from people with nothing better to do. Just learn to ignore the unwarranted opinions as you will do with the unwarranted advice. This is true whether you feel depressed or crazy or bored, or anything else to be honest. It is simply nobody else's business: the only person you need to listen to is yourself.

- Keep calm
- Trust your instinct
- Listen to the baby expert: YOU

Chapter 6
Your Body After Baby
– What to Expect

E ven though every waking second of your life is now spent thinking about your baby, you're still allowed to worry about your sagging tummy and lazy bladder.

Although your baby is now the centre of your universe, you will still have innumerable concerns about yourself and your weird post-baby body. And that's okay. Even if you are a 100 per cent focused super-mum, it doesn't stop you being miffed about the way your bottom now appears to 'hang'.

It's absolutely vital to look after yourself after you've had your baby, both physically and mentally. Why shouldn't you? Being a mummy expert involves prioritising your needs as well as her majesty's. And there's no guilt in that. A vital part of enjoying parenthood is about being comfortable in yourself: and you can't get comfortable if you're stuck with a floppy pelvic floor, so you've got to sort it.

A little word of caution before you even think about your body: there are many falsehoods and myths in the parenting world – old-wives' tales and other bunkum. A particularly silly one is the magic 'six weeks', which is supposed to be the time that everything falls into place with you and your baby. The routine, the sleeping, the feeding: rumour has it that it's all sorted by six weeks. Apparently, exercise, life, sex can all start again at six weeks. Really?

I don't know who coined the six-week magic window myth, but I do know they'd probably never had a baby or lived on planet Earth. I'm sorry to break the magic spell, but there is no magic six weeks when suddenly everything pings into place physically. In real life, where most of us live, once you've had a baby things settle down very gradually and the idea of a six-week target is hogwash. Things calm down at all different times, often after six weeks, sometimes before.

Yes, some babies are 'settled' by six weeks and some mummies are back in the gym. But we are all different and getting your body sorted, never mind the baby, takes time. Don't forget you have been pregnant for the better part of a year: it'll take more than an hour or two to recover.

And then there are the pictures of celeb-mummies back in skinny jeans five minutes after giving birth. I actually saw a photo in a magazine the other day of a celebrity shopping *one* day after she had given birth! What is that all about? I have no idea (incidentally, I also had no idea who she was). I'm sorry but no one in the real world looks like the Duchess of Cambridge after giving birth.

Of course, competitive mummies will be dying to show you their honed stretch-mark-free abdomen at the first opportunity. But keep calm: for us real women, it can take quite a while to feel physically normal. Being realistic about that means you'll keep calm and not feel like some enormous failure when you're still in maternity jeans after a month or two (or six).

Rather than giving you an encyclopaedic list of all the physical changes you'll notice after giving birth, this chapter covers the kind of things I am asked about, week in week out, by *real* women. I want to make you aware of the real-life worries that mums have about their postnatal bodies rather than any definitive list of postnatal medical complications. That explains why there's a big chunk on weight.

- Keep calm
- Listen to your body
- Trust your instinct

Shedding those pounds

There is nothing complicated about losing weight after you've had a baby: it certainly is *not* rocket science. In fact, it's terribly basic with a very simple idea that applies at all other times: the calories you burn have to exceed the calories you eat. Simple, right?

Wrong! The theory is exactly the same, yes, but the reality is hugely different from losing weight pre-baby. There are about 45 reasons for this, the main ones being:

- All-consuming exhaustion
- Hormones
- Lack of time
- There seems to be a lot more weight than before!
- The flabby bits are in new places
- You're at least a year older

This makes the whole post-birth weight-loss issue rather tricky. So while the idea is very simple, actually losing baby weight is far from simple.

As well as a calorie deficit, getting back into your jeans requires time, patience and a little bit of realism. Whichever plan has worked for you before, whether you were a calorie counter or a gym-bunny, will work again I assure you, but it is just going to take longer.

There is no magic solution to losing weight: no pill or potion, or highly over-priced regime. What will work is something that is practical with your new lifestyle and something you can enjoy. Now is not the time to be suffering a strict crash diet or drinking slop rather than eating food. Post-baby weight comes off slowly with a sensible, easy-to-follow approach: it will not be a quick fix.

Providing you are patient and realistic about your new timetable, something will work. Sensible slimming clubs work as long as you can get to the meetings and they take into account your breastfeeding and postnatal needs. Simply calorie counting also works, if you are careful not to be too restrictive and you don't drive yourself mad: it's hassle enough scooping out formula and puréed veg for your baby, never mind weighing out morsels of food for yourself. You have to be honest with yourself about what you can be bothered with, so you're not in for a huge disappointment. The slow, measured approach will be the easiest and the most successful.

Crash, fad diets never work for anyone because of the rebound hunger. They are particularly bad after you've had a baby when you need the energy and enjoyment from food. Choose a plan that has worked for you before, and that you truly believe will work as opposed to some foolish idea from the internet. Do not be conned by ads for crazy pills, and weird teas that claim to shift baby-tummies: they are designed for one purpose only, and that purpose is to make someone (not you) very rich. If these wacky things worked, we wouldn't have the current obesity crisis.

There is no right or wrong time to start thinking about losing weight. When your body can cope without that giant bar of Dairy Milk after lunch is more than likely the right time. Be guided by you and only you: there is not a magic deadline you must start by; it depends on your energy levels and how you're feeling mentally. I'd be amazed if this happens before your baby is three months old, but for some super-human mummies it starts earlier. I was far too comfortable in my maternity jeans and didn't even consider any concerted effort until much later.

You can lose weight when breastfeeding: many mummies find breastfeeding actually helps with weight loss, but don't fret if it doesn't for you. Breastfeeding obviously uses up calories and you have to be very careful about making sure you are eating enough calories for both of you. A diet that is rich in first-class wholesome real food is going to be good for you and healthy for your baby, so neither of you will miss out on essential nutrients.

Exercise is obviously a fantastic way to lose weight and a fabulous stress-relief, but there's only one, rather large, fly in the ointment with that: the BABY! Indeed, it's not as easy to go out for a jog or to the gym four times a week when you've got your baby in tow. That is why you have to be reasonable and honest with yourself. It's unlikely, at this stage in your life, that you're going to get to the gym several times a week, so don't set yourself up for failure. Once or twice a week may be possible depending on your set-up and which willing victim will look after your baby for an hour. If the whole plan is a stress-inducing hassle, it's just not going to happen. That's fine: try a plan that's destined to work, not doomed to fail.

Come up with a sensible, workable schedule that admittedly may take longer to have any massive impact on your massive belly, but will work in the long run. Don't forget you can also exercise with your little one: pushing her buggy is great exercise, and you might even find it easier to walk places sometimes rather than load her and all her gear into the car. Once or twice a week for 'proper' solo exercise is possibly do-able and would be a great regime for anyone, never mind someone with a new body and a new baby to think about. (I'd be happy if I could get all my patients to do that whether they've had a baby or not.)

If you do get this chance, choose a type of exercise you've done before. Now is not the time to sample a kettle bell workout if you don't even know what a kettle bell is.

Habitual exercise-junkies can safely go back to old regimes with the thumbs-up of their doctor, but if exercise was not your norm before you had your baby, play it safe by choosing gentle exercise such as walking and swimming that will burn the calories without traumatising your already fragile new body.

You have to be more cautious with the exercise if you've had a Caesarean. When you have a section, the muscles holding in your tummy have been cut and need time and patience to heal well. Vigorous cardio exercise or abdominal workouts are only to be tried gently, once you've had the go-ahead at your six-week check. Whenever you begin, start slowly to avoid straining those sore tummy muscles.

You don't have to even think about weight loss if you don't want to. But I know from the mummies I see each week in clinic that it's really essential to a lot of you and there's no shame in that. I don't expect you to be in the gym three days after delivery: I am certainly no body fascist and I genuinely don't care how people look. But likewise if *you* care about the way you look and feel, then you should try to make the effort for your own self-esteem, so you feel fabulous mentally and physically. You should empower yourself to do that if it is what you want, and there is absolutely no guilt in that. Wanting to look good, or look like your 'old' self, is perfectly normal and natural, and if that feels right to you, then listen to yourself and do it.

Your perineum

The chances are before you got pregnant or gave birth you wouldn't have even heard or said the word *perineum*. You would certainly never have discussed it in polite company, and you wouldn't have been concerned about its functioning or whereabouts. But I can guarantee after giving birth, you will definitely know where it is and right now you're probably feeling positively protective of it.

The perineum is like a sling of muscle, a bit like a hammock but less swingy, that houses your urethra, your vagina and your rectum. It is holding everything in place and keeping control of what comes in and what comes out. Even though you won't have discussed it much before, if ever, it's a rather crucial area of your anatomy, especially for women who care about their sex life and weeing at the right time. When people talk about your pelvic floor, this is what they mean.

Without a doubt your perineum takes a battering during labour and birth. Okay, let's be honest 'takes a battering' is probably an understatement: it has pretty much been in the Blitz. Stretched, bruised, torn, cut, stitched, poked, prodded: it's all been torture for that poor pelvic floor of yours so if you're feeling a bit fragile down there, do not be surprised.

It can certainly take a few weeks for it to feel remotely like it did before, and if you've had stitches even longer for the scar tissue to settle and soften. Within a couple of weeks of giving birth, you shouldn't still have actual pain

– if you do, consult your GP. Continuing pain can be a sign of infection or poor healing so it's not to be ignored.

The reason doctors harp on about pelvic floor exercises is so you can regain strength in that poor perineum of yours and hold on to that all-important bladder control. You may have noticed going for a wee is slightly 'easier' than before and 100 per cent control doesn't come back straight away. This is normal in the first few weeks.

Absolutely the funniest thing that ever happened to me after having children was the day a midwife told me I needed the incontinence clinic, and my husband and I laughed so much I did actually wet myself. I had given birth to a 7.5 lb baby only 48 hours earlier and here I was being written a prescription for Tena Lady because I admitted I didn't have 100 per cent control of my bladder. Luckily, it was my second child and I saw the funny side: had someone told me that after my first baby, I actually would have believed them, and gone out to buy a plastic bedsheet.

In the first few days, you will not have complete control of your bladder, but you don't need the incontinence clinic at this stage. This should all gradually start to improve, and your wee control should get back to normal within two or three months.

Here comes a rule: if dry knickers are important to you, you *have* to do pelvic floor exercises to help strengthen your muscles. This does not mean having a quick squeeze now and then, when you remember. This means a concerted effort, every day, right from the start. Set an alarm on your phone and be dedicated. A proper pelvic floor exercise involves holding in an imaginary wee and an imaginary poo at the same time: trying this means you will be concentrating on the right muscles. You should do these repeated 'squeezes' for little sessions of five minutes throughout the day. When you've become an expert, you can start to hold in your tummy muscles at the same time for added pelvic floor power. This is essential whether you had a vaginal birth or a Caesarean.

Pooing and piles

So while we're on the subject of your pelvic floor, there's also your back passage to think about, which right now probably also feels like it's been in World War Three. Although it's not strictly *involved* in the whole birth process, it certainly gets caught in the cross-fire and if you have had a tear or a cut (an episiotomy) this will affect control of your rectum.

In the first few days after birth, pooing will certainly not be an enjoyable experience and you will have to take it easy. Constipation is a nightmare at this stage because opening your bowels can be quite sore, but much worse if what comes out is very hard. Send someone down to the shops to get you plenty of poo-softening fruit such as peaches, plums, prunes and dried fruit, and make sure you are drinking plenty of water. If you can keep everything soft, your bottom will heal a lot easier and going to the loo will no longer seem so scary.

Like everything else, with time this will stop being so

painful and should start to feel normal. At any stage if pooing doesn't feel 'right' or you feel it's more painful than it should be, head to the GP. That is what we are there for, and no good GP would be surprised to see you with this really common issue. We are very used to talking about poo (as you soon will be too) and it's important to sort this out.

Piles really are a pain in the backside (sorry, couldn't resist). Piles or haemorrhoids are so common in pregnancy and afterwards, I'm surprised if women say they *don't* have them. Whether you've had a normal or a Caesarean birth, you are prone to them because of the weight of the baby in your womb during pregnancy. This pushes on the veins around your back passage, which swell and bulge and form piles. Piles feel itchy and usually throb, and when you wipe your bottom you may feel squidgy hangy bits that weren't there before. They often bleed, particularly after you've been to the loo.

As long as you avoid constipation, piles can settle down in the first two or three months after birth, otherwise it's a trip to the GP please. Avoiding straining when you need the toilet is the key to letting them calm down. The creams and suppositories you can buy in the chemist can relieve some of the discomfort.

Sex and contraception

After the battering your perineum has taken, sex may well be the last thing on your mind. But at some point, whether it's a few weeks or a few months down the line, it will be back on the agenda. There are no instructions dictating when you can or can't jump back into bed and given the crazy, hazy first few weeks it may not be top of your to-do list for a while. But plenty of women I come across do have sex in the first few weeks after giving birth, because they feel comfortable and ready. That is how you know when it's right: you will just feel like it. There is no deadline or specific date; this is all about you and your partner. No rules.

Your sex life is not a thing of the past just because you've given birth. In fact, sex is a great activity once you become parents, as it doesn't require a babysitter, it's free and it needs no forward planning (your other half is quite likely to agree). Of course you spend a lot of time shattered, and at the outset you will be understandably nervous, but you should soon be back in the swing of things. It should still be as fun and enjoyable as before. The notion that people stop having sex when they become parents isn't really true, otherwise my antenatal clinics would be empty.

Sex after birth should not feel painful. Perhaps uncomfortable the first or second time, but pain is not normal, and warrants a chat with your GP. After birth, particularly if you are breastfeeding, weirdly the levels of the female hormone oestrogen actually drop. It doesn't really sound right given this is a time you're embracing femininity and Mother Nature, but it's true. When oestrogen drops, your vagina and vulva can feel very dry and not particularly ready for action. This is perfectly normal and is simply a phase for a few months, when you will find it helps to use a lubricant.

As you have recently discovered, sex makes babies. I hope this does not come as new information. Do not be under any false impression that sex after birth is any different. Put quite simply, if you don't want to get pregnant, use contraception.

Contrary to popular belief you can get pregnant when you are breastfeeding and you can get pregnant before your periods return to normal. Sure, breastfeeding does reduce your chances as it is mildly contraceptive, but if you're adamant you don't want a second child right now, don't take the risk. Breastfeeding is not a reliable contraceptive so make sure you sort out an alternative, superior one. This should be discussed at your six-week check: if you can't decide what to use at this stage, just have some condoms to hand so you're prepared. I have come across more than one family with an 11-month age gap between siblings: if that's not for you, get yourself organised!

While we're in this area, a word or two about bleeding. It can be normal to bleed after birth for anything up to six weeks. This *lochia* as it's called should really feel like an extended period, bright and red at the start then going into a more prolonged phase of brown discharge. At the beginning there can be a lot of blood (you will understand why maternity pads are so hefty), which can come as quite a surprise. If at any point it feels like it's too much, or getting heavier rather than lighter, you should have a chat to your midwife as it can be a sign of infection.

Stretch marks

The great myth about stretch marks is that someone has an answer to getting rid of them. The actual truth about stretch marks is that they fade over time and their existence is simply down to your genes and your skin type.

Stretch marks are a natural phenomenon of pregnancy. They are exactly what they claim to be – marks on your skin from where you've stretched. In the first few weeks after giving birth they look pretty angry, red and are very obvious: you've got a newly saggy belly and if that wasn't awful enough, it's got zig-zag camouflage stripes all over it. Doesn't make you feel great, does it?

Firstly, I can assure you that however awful they may look now, any stretch marks will improve over the next few months. Eventually they will fade to your normal skin tone, and just blend in. There are plenty of oils, creams and magic potions you can buy that will claim to have the answer to stretch marks. I once met a woman who rubbed breast milk into her stretch marks: she felt it moisturised them and improved the way they looked. Whether or not you try that is entirely up to you – I am certainly not advocating it, but the reality is no one has the answer to stretch marks.

But there is no harm in rubbing cream in, is there? Of course there isn't, as long as you've not been conned into spending this month's mortgage payment on a cream that is supposed to rid you of stretch marks. There is no potion that can do that. Believe me if there was we'd all know about it, and all be using it.

I see a lot of tummies in my job – fat ones, thin ones,

dark ones, pale ones, wobbly ones, pierced ones: all sorts. And I have seen stretch marks on all of types of bellies and all types of bodies. And legs, and bottoms for that matter. I can honestly tell you that having stretch marks has very little to do with what you have put on your skin, and a great deal to do with your own skin type.

I only have one stretch mark on my far-from-flat tummy after two pregnancies and I can honestly say I never really had the patience or time for creaming myself religiously. I have certainly never been one for buying expensive lotions. On the other hand patients of mine have had stretch marks despite spending fortunes on celebrity-endorsed creams. Please don't be conned into doing this. You have far better things to spend your money on, I'm sure.

Moisturising your skin, with even the most basic of creams, is obviously a good idea, as it makes your skin feel nicer and more supple. It may improve the way the stretch marks look but it won't rid you of them – you'll just have to be patient and wait for them to fade naturally.

Hair loss

Just when you're feeling like you've got this baby-lark sorted and your body is starting to vaguely resemble something you recognise as yours, your hair starts to fall out. Well, thank you Mother Nature, that's just what us girls wanted.

Losing your hair is absolutely normal in the few months after you've given birth. Most mummies complain to me about this when their babies are around three or four months old, when you'll notice the shower is clogged with hair and your brush seems to be full of it.

We all shed hair all the time as part of the normal cycle of its growth, but while you're pregnant very little hair falls out, which is why you feel all Rapunzel-esque with luxuriant tresses. After the birth, as your hair returns to its normal growing and shedding pattern, you notice usual shedding plus the extra left over from pregnancy. This combines to make a pretty noticeable hair loss, but it soon settles down. It should not be falling out in patches or clumps, just more hairs in the brush than normal. You don't need any special shampoo or supplements to help with this. It is completely par for the course and will settle down.

You will notice your locks are less voluminous than they were pre-birth, but it shouldn't be a shocking change. If it does feel like too much, you should certainly mention it to your GP. Hair loss can be a symptom of anaemia (see below), but also an underactive thyroid, which is a common problem after pregnancy. Sometimes hair loss is the only symptom of these conditions, so it's not to be ignored. Do not be embarrassed to speak to your GP about this; this is not a vanity issue, it is genuinely important.

Anaemia

Being shattered after giving birth is normal and it is expected for a few months. All new parents feel exhausted and gradually as you get your slumber-filled nights back, this should start to improve.

It is, however, really important to notice if you feel 'more-than' tired. Now this may sound difficult to gauge given you've never been so sleep-deprived in your life, but believe me you will notice if you are overly fatigued.

Being excessively tired after giving birth can be sign of having low iron levels, which is called anaemia. This is *very* common in pregnancy and afterwards, and it's important to sort out. Being anaemic not only worsens tiredness, it also slows down healing and worsens other delightful postnatal issues, such as depression (see page 91) and hair loss (see above).

Anaemia is really simple to diagnose with a blood test and is certainly worth it if you are feeling excessively tired. If you are anaemic, you will be advised to replace all that iron you've used up in the pregnancy with iron supplements prescribed by your doctor. These are pretty effective at reversing the anaemia and ending that awful feeling of being bashed over the head by a mallet. Eating iron-rich foods is a great idea for anyone after birth, but it is unlikely to reverse anaemia unless you tend to eat a bag of broccoli a day.

- Keep calm
- Trust your instinct
- Listen to the baby expert: YOU

Chapter 7
Let's Talk About Poo
– Yes, Really ...

Yes, this book has an entire chapter on poo. I studied medicine at Cambridge University with a cohort of exceptionally clever people. Many of my contemporaries are at the forefront of clinical research and medical science. They publish research on things like synapses, mitochondria, polymorphism and enoyl-acyl carrier proteins (don't worry, I don't know what they are either). On the other hand, I have written a book with a whole chapter dedicated to poo.

The reason I have done this is because I have realised over the past few years that most new mummies and daddies want to hear all about it. Given half the chance, a new mum won't hesitate to give me details of her little one's latest nappy offering. At the six-week check, I always ask a new mum if her baby's bowel movements are okay and, honestly, a simple yes or no would suffice. But no! I get all the intricacies: colour, smell, quantity, timings. On extra-special occasions parents will even bring dirty nappies in to show me. Such a treat. I have even seen photo albums with documented evidence of baby's first poo. We are a funny lot.

Many new parents are fascinated, interested, worried and often positively obsessed with their baby's poo, and to be honest it accounts for a good number of consultations I have. Never in your life will you talk about poo so much or so liberally as after you've had a baby. (You just have to remember when you go back to having conversations with *normal* people, it isn't quite so acceptable.)

Parents have absolutely no hesitation in asking me about their children's bowel movements in the clinic and, to be honest, anywhere else. I was once at a two-year-old's birthday party with my daughter, filling up on fairy cakes and enjoying the organised chaos. A lady who I had spoken to probably once in my life came up to me and said, 'Oh, you're a doctor aren't you? Can I ask you a question?' Now, I get this a lot as you can imagine and, actually, because I'm inherently curious (read nosey) I usually say, yes. So, she pointed out her two-year-old daughter on the floor, and said, 'Do you think it's normal she does adult-sized poos? I mean, they're the same size as my husband's ...' As much as I like talking about children's poo, I was rather scared where that conversation was heading, so we skipped birthday cake and ran off before I got a complete rundown of stool size in her extended family.

So everyone wants to discuss their child's bowels. Fewer people mention to me their husband's. Healthy pooing is a sign of a healthy baby so I'm always happy to hear about it. A 'normal' poo tells you a lot about a baby: he's feeding well, healthy and happy. And, joking aside, poos can cause a little bit of anxiety: 'Are they the right colour?', 'Does he do them often enough?', 'What actually is normal?', 'My friend's baby poos more often than mine!' Oh yes, I've heard that one more than once. Even pooing can set competitive mummies off on a rant. So poo does warrant a whole chapter.

Are there rules on poo?

Thankfully, no. There probably is some dogma doing the rounds about when and how your baby *should* be pooing, but in reality there are genuinely no rules here. There are some vague parameters of what is normal, but you must remember there is a huge spectrum when it comes to baby's poo in the first year. You will get to know what is normal for your unique pooper. Probably the only useful guide here is to know that if there is a change in your baby's pooping habits, it *may* suggest a problem. However, there will be times when changes in pooing habits are expected, especially when your baby's diet changes from breast to bottle, or when you start weaning him on to solids (see Chapter 11) or giving him cow's milk at a year old.

So how often is normal for a baby to open his bowels? How long is a piece of string? The answer is that every baby is different (just like every adult) and how often a baby poos is really not that significant. What is important is that he is gloriously happy pooing, with no tears, and what comes out is nice and soft. Pooing should be a comfortable experience. That doesn't mean your baby can't be squeezing or pushing a little bit, but that he should not be in any discomfort as he delivers the goods.

A gastroenterology professor I trained with taught me that people should enjoy opening their bowels as much as they enjoy a good meal. I think you have to be a gastroenterology professor to appreciate that. You get the message, though: pooing should be satisfying, not distressing.

I often meet perfectly contented, healthy breastfed babies who poop once a week. This is fantastically economical from a nappy perspective. Likewise, other contented, healthy breastfed babies will poo with every feed, particularly when they are first born. This can be thanks to their very efficient 'gastrocolic reflex': once something goes into his tummy, something's gotta come out!

Normal breastfed baby poo tends to be soft and maybe even runny. People always say breastfed poo should look like mustard. This is fine if like me you have Dijon mustard in your house, but rather misleading if you have wholegrain mustard. It is normal for breastfed poo to have little pale bits in it that look like bits of cottage cheese (but not mustard seeds). It's funny – if you made all these food references in relation to adult bowels, people would be completely disgusted, but like I said, anything goes when talking about baby poo.

If your baby is formula-fed, he will do quite firm poos, almost like a paste. They should still be soft and therefore easy to push out. They are a paler brown than your standard adult poo, which is what you would expect given your baby's only intake is milk. It is fair to say you'll be pretty surprised/impressed/horrified/intrigued by the smell of a formula poo, which can be rather potent. In general, I find formula-fed babies open their bowels every day, probably because their poos are that bit bulkier.

Once you start weaning your baby, obviously what goes in is going to affect what comes out. So you're in for a right treat. Once your baby is eating solids, his poo will smell much more, get darker and tend to be harder, but still no huge effort or discomfort should be required to get it out. How many dirty nappies you see a week will start to fluctuate according to what your baby has eaten as well as how much he is moving around: once he's crawling you'll notice how exercise gets his bowels moving! (The same is true for adults by the way, in case you're in need of any assistance in that department.)

So really, the only rule for poo is that babies should be at ease pooing, and it shouldn't cause any distress or great effort. If your baby is calm filling his nappy, you can keep calm.

GRrrrrrrrr

I often have parents coming to see me worried that their little one is constipated because of that noise babies have a habit of making. You've probably already heard it and thought, 'What's that all about?' It sounds a bit like groaning and pushing, but with no crying or discomfort. If you were pretending to strain, it's the noise you'd make. It's basically how you think babies would look if they were doing a poo, except it often results in an empty nappy.

This is where it causes concern, as parents assume their little 'un is trying to push something out unsuccessfully.

If your baby is doing that straining *I-look-like-I'm-pooing* thing but he's not in discomfort, and having regular soft poos, then he is *not* constipated. You will know yourself if your baby seems distressed: this groaning noise alone does not indicate distress. All babies do this – it is quite normal.

The pushing business often happens actually when babies are pushing wind out; it is a natural phenomenon for babies to strain against gas in their lower bowel. Babies can't tell the difference between wind and poo in their rectum, so strain against all of it. Thankfully, it's something they grow out of well before you potty-train them. Going various shades of red when pooing is also perfectly normal and not a symptom of distress or discomfort. It's merely a cue for you to get the changing mat out, and hand your baby over to Daddy.

- Trust your instinct: you will know if the poo is right
- You are already a poo expert
- Keep calm if you have a calm pooper

Nappy contents that aren't normal

All babies, both breastfed and bottle-fed, before and after weaning, will produce abnormal poo, caused by factors such as viruses, different foods and life in general.

To judge 'abnormal' listen to your instinct and how you feel your baby is in himself. What is normal for your baby and does he seem fine to you? Trust yourself, and if you are the slightest bit worried, get some medical advice.

I would say all abnormal poo warrants at least a discussion with your GP, if not a fully blown consultation. But there is not always a need to panic. If your baby has one loose stool in a day of otherwise normal ones and good feeding, you don't need to fret. It is when there is a consistent change, or you feel instinctively something is not right, that you should seek advice.

Going to speak to your GP or health visitor about your baby's bowel movements is perfectly normal and expected, and not something you should feel remotely hesitant about. It is a completely normal thing for us to hear about and it can tell us a lot about what's going on with your little one. Any symptom or concern that is important to YOU is important to us, so we want to hear about it. Your GP is there to support you after you've had a baby and should never make you feel embarrassed or that you're a time-waster if you have a concern about your baby. That is what we are here for.

I have included a list of abnormal nappy contents, below, which you are very welcome to stick on the fridge unless you care what your in-laws might think.

The aim of this list is *not* so you can diagnose what is going on. The aim is to flag what should concern you enough to instigate a discussion with your GP. You can google these things and get a whole host of scary causes that will frighten the life out of you. Or you can chat it through with a healthcare professional, who will assess your baby properly and come up with a proper diagnosis.

In the main, abnormal poos in babies are not caused by scary conditions such as bowel disease. Be reassured that if something unusual was happening, you would notice other problems such as not growing, not feeding, and strange patterns of sleeping and crying.

NAPPY CONTENTS	SHOULD I WORRY?	WHAT MIGHT BE GOING ON?
Blood	Yes. Blood is never normal so you must speak to your GP.	• Infection • Constipation • Food allergy or intolerance
Mucus	No, but speak to your GP.	• Infection • Allergy • Drooling and teething
Green poo	No, but if it lasts longer than one poo speak to your GP or health visitor.	• Breastfeeding habits • Type of formula • Infection
Diarrhoea	No, but speak to your GP as your baby is in danger of dehydration.	• Infection • Food intolerance • Too much fruit • Antibiotics
Pellety rabbit droppings	No, but it sounds like your baby is constipated	• Constipation
Large, hard poos	No, but it sounds like your baby is constipated	• Constipation

Many people claim teething causes diarrhoea. In fact, teething causes slightly looser poo, which can be very acidic and lead to nappy rash. Strictly speaking, if your baby has diarrhoea you shouldn't really assume it is simply from teething, unless it is normal teething behaviour you have seen before. Teething classically causes rosy cheeks, lots of dribbling and a desire to chew *anything*. Be guided by your instinct: unless you're confident from other signs that your baby is teething, get him checked out by your GP when he has diarrhoea.

Even stranger things to see in poos

Somebody very sensible once said 'what goes in must come out'. I have no idea what on earth they were referring to specifically, but I can assure you that once you wean your baby on to solid food (see Chapter 11) you will completely understand this statement.

When you are weaning your baby, his little bowel doesn't always fully digest what he's eaten. This is especially true with fruits or vegetables that are very high in fibre. That means what you pop in one end can literally reappear pretty much unscathed out the other end. It can come as rather a surprise when you spy a first nappy-raisin but do not be alarmed! Foods notorious for appearing in nappies include:

- Carrots: you can't fail to recognise that bright-orange poo.
- Raisins: these usually come out completely untouched.

- Blueberries: the skin comes straight through and stains everything black.

Baked beans appear too and even sometimes the thready, fibrous bits from the inside of a banana. A doctor friend of mine once saw those stringy things in his baby son's nappy and freaked out thinking the poor thing had worms. Luckily his wife was more sensible than him and knew exactly what was going on.

Finding these foods in your baby's nappies does not mean you have to stop giving them; fibre is great for babies' and toddlers' bowels and it's fabulous for them to develop an appetite for fibrous foods. As your baby grows older and his bowel matures, the nappy-raisins will disappear.

What is constipation?

Pooing once every few days in a perfectly chilled-out baby is normal. Constipation, on the other hand, means hard, uncomfortable poos that don't appear very often.

Constipation is a big deal. It's a really common problem that doesn't only affect poo-time. Being bunged up with poo makes you feel pretty rough all day long, whether you're six months old or 36 years old, so it's worth sorting out.

Identifying constipation in babies involves looking for the key signs, but as a super-mamma expert you won't need any checklist of signs. I can assure you, it will be pretty clear to you if your baby is constipated because he just won't seem like himself. You are the best person in the world to judge this, and you will feel he is not right. He will be uncomfortable when he's trying to poo and generally irritable and fed up. Signs of constipation in babies include:

- Pain/distress when filling a nappy.
- Large, hard poos.
- Small quantities of pellet poo that resemble rabbit poo.
- Very infrequent dirty nappies with pain, irritability or discomfort (so a once-a-week pooper who is perfectly content is nothing to worry about!)

So what is actually going on? Well, we don't always know why the poo doesn't appear easily. As with adults, some babies just have a tendency towards constipation and there is not an obvious cause.

Constipation in exclusively breastfed babies is unusual as breast milk is a laxative. That doesn't mean it can't happen, though, sometimes for no apparent reason at all. Factors such as hot weather or reduced feeding can cause poos to get a bit dehydrated and difficult to push out.

Babies who are mixed-fed or formula-fed can sometimes be constipated and it may feel right to you to switch formula (see below) to see if that gets things moving. Certain brands do seem to be bulkier and a simple brand-switch can sort everything out.

Once you've weaned your baby and solids make up a significant proportion of his diet, his little bowels are getting used to a whole range of foods, some of which can be constipating so that's definitely worth thinking about. Don't drive yourself potty (couldn't resist) looking for the reason why your baby is constipated. He may just have a tendency towards slow bowel movements. What is important is trying to solve it so that your baby learns to enjoy pooing and isn't suffering with all that straining. You're a couple of years away from potty-training, but even from a very young age pooing should be a joyous experience for your baby.

- Keep calm
- Trust yourself to find a solution
- Do not feel guilty: constipation is no one's 'fault'

What can I do, my baby won't poo?

Like that wise old bloke said, 'What goes in must come out.' Thinking about what's going in the top end may help to sort out the bottom end. It is worth having a look at these possible solutions, as a simple change can make all the difference to your baby.

- **Water intake** Put simply, in order to make soft, easy-to-pass poos, lots of water needs to be available in the bowel. When babies are exclusively milk-fed, although their diet is only fluid, surprisingly they may still need some extra water. This can happen when the weather is warmer or some babies will need this extra water all the time, simply to ease their bowel movements. You can offer your baby cooled, boiled water from a bottle or a sterilised spoon to increase water intake. A newish baby may only take 5 or 10 ml from a spoon, whereas a baby of three or more months may take as much as 50–60 ml throughout the day between feeds. There is really no right or wrong way – it's what works for you and your baby. Many parents I see find this is just enough to get the poo that bit softer and ease constipation: mums have been doing this for centuries because it works.

- **Switching formula** I don't generally recommend that people switch formula brand, especially once their baby is settled on a certain taste. However, the type of formula milk you are using may be causing those rock-hard poos. Now, this doesn't make perfect sense, as they are a 'formula', and they should really all be the same, but this is the reality: some brands are just known to create tough poos. I have seen many mummies switch brand and ease the hard poo issue. Watch out too for those formulas that claim to be more suited to ravenous babies; they can make rock-hard poos as they are generally bulkier. If this could be an issue, think about whether or not the bulkier formula is necessary: some mums start on this for little reason when a straightforward formula would be perfectly fine.

- **Fruits for poo** Once a baby has started solids you will see huge changes in bowel movements in terms of frequency, size, texture and smell (smell always gets the dads talking). Right from the start of weaning, babies eat a variety of fruit regularly and that is particularly useful if your baby is tending towards constipation. Most fruits are laxatives, but there are miracle ones that are particularly good as they contain a high concentration of a natural sugar called sorbitol. Sorbitol makes easily moved soft poos. Ensuring your baby is eating a mushy variety of these daily as part of his weaning diet can help to prevent constipation. Remember the P fruits for pooing: Peaches, Plums, Prunes, Pears, aPricots – easy to remember as they all contain the letter P for poo.

- **Bananas for bananas** Most babies love soft, mushy banana – it's a fabulous weaning fruit and an all-round brilliant food. Except if you're constipated. Bananas solidify poops making them a great help if baby has diarrhoea but something to avoid if he's struggling to poo.

If none of these things help with your baby's constipation, it is certainly worth getting advice from your GP.

And what about diarrhoea?

Diarrhoea is very runny or watery poos, coming much more often and usually in larger quantities than normal. It is *not* one slightly looser poo in a day of good ones. It is not the diarrhoea itself that's a worry, but all that fluid your baby is pooing out. Always take your baby to the GP if he has diarrhoea as he will need to be medically assessed.

The concern with any baby under one with diarrhoea is

dehydration, which can happen surprisingly quickly. It doesn't take many watery poos for babies to lose a substantial amount of their total body fluids, so a medical consultation is essential for diarrhoea – that is actually a rule on poo that is worth heeding.

Nappy rash

You can't really talk about poo without talking about nappy rash. Every baby at some stage of babyhood will get nappy rash. Some lucky ones get it once or twice only. Others seem to have it every month. This is just part of the wonderful spectrum of babies: there is certainly no 'normal' when it comes to derrieres. Some botties are incredibly robust and can handle diarrhoea and wee, and a forgotten nappy change, and still be peachy and perfect. Others are far more precious, needing TLC and pristine cleanliness at all times to avoid a rash.

Nappy rash is basically skin that is irritated and inflamed from being in contact with something it doesn't like for too long. Usual causes would be diarrhoea or wee. Babies tend to have worse nappy rash when they are unwell otherwise, and you may also notice it worsens during teething. Once you've started weaning, you'll probably see that some fruits worsen nappy rash, and that's because the fruit is making acidic poop.

There will be 'rules' that state that you can avoid nappy rash by changing your baby's nappy regularly. Well, I don't think that's always the case so that's another failed rule destined to make mummies feels guilty. Yes, sometimes nappy rash can be caused by not changing a baby's nappy often enough, but it does not automatically mean you have failed at one aspect of parenting. Of course you should change your baby's nappy regularly, but being fastidious about changing doesn't prevent nappy rash in every baby: some just have more sensitive skin that is prone to getting nappy rash. And nappy rash is certainly no reflection of your parenting prowess: so let's bin any guilt and concentrate on sorting it.

What rashy-botties need for recovery is to be left alone from whatever's bugging them so they can enjoy the dryness. There are two completely easy ways to achieve this:

1. Get the nappy off: this lets air in and keeps irritating factors out. Your baby can lie on his changing mat instead of his playmat, sit playing on the bathroom floor for half an hour or on any floor that can be mopped. If you're clever, you'll choose a non-pooing time. The worst that will happen is there's a baby-wee on the floor. In the grand scheme of what you've dealt with thus far, that's not too traumatic. And baby-wees are tiny.

2. Slap on loads of cream. Nappy rash needs barrier cream not moisturiser. The idea of the cream is to form a protective layer, so that the skin can heal itself underneath. Get a nappy cream or barrier cream from your pharmacist – apply it every time you change your baby's nappy and use double the amount at bedtime.

Nappy rash should heal really quickly in 3–4 days, otherwise it's a chat with the GP please. If it looks very sore, weepy or you're just not happy with it, head down to the surgery earlier. If your little one gets nappy rash often, then use cream all the time until his botty gets tougher. I don't think it's necessary for the average baby, though. Use your instinct and do what you want. Are you a terrible mother if your baby's bottom is fine so you don't regularly use nappy cream? Of course you're not.

There are plenty of questions (and rules!) around the use of baby wipes on babies' bums: Should you use them? What age? Are they bad for the skin? Here is how you will answer this question for yourself: you'll start using water and cotton wool on your baby's bum when he's a newborn, then gradually, through necessity, discover that wipes are easier. This will happen spontaneously when there's a poo explosion everywhere, you're out, you're in a hurry, you're tired, Grandad's changing him, or it's the middle of the night. And if his bott is fine with that, you'll have sanctioned your own rule on wipes: they're fine for your baby. My guess is if and when you have a fourth baby you won't even start with the cotton wool: that might not be what the 'rules' say, but it's the reality, tried-and-tested by mummies. We all end up doing this.

- Keep calm
- Trust your instinct
- Listen to the baby expert: YOU

Chapter 8
Baby Development – It's Not A Competition

There is something quite weird that happens the moment that double blue line appears on the pregnancy test. Well, yes, there are a lot of weird things that happen, but most of them are expected. This one I think less so. An area of our brain springs to life that lay dormant before: *the competitive-mum lobe*. Suddenly, without realising, women who have never before been concerned about the achievements and assets of the sisterhood, start comparing themselves to every other pregnant woman and every other mum. And once it starts, it probably doesn't ever stop. The moment your baby is born, that part of your brain goes into super-sized overdrive.

From my own experience, and the lovely mummies I look after, I acknowledge it is absolutely impossible as a mum not to compare your baby to others; it's completely normal to feel smug when your little one is the first to do a high-five and to feel downright deflated when she's the only one not clapping.

Us women don't make it easy for ourselves by constantly comparing and parading our babies. I genuinely think this is a natural, inherent phenomenon. No one would choose to do it: it's this competitive-mum lobe that annoyingly has survived natural selection. It leads us down a pathway of rivalry and contest, and there is no greater outlet for this than your antenatal group, AKA your *mummy-gang*.

Comparing notes

On many levels antenatal classes are fatally flawed. I am sorry to say this, but it's true and chances are if you've given birth by now, you'll agree with me. Generally they prepare you for birth (if you're lucky), while totally failing to prepare you for parenthood. You learn the intricacies of pain relief, while learning nothing about looking after your baby. However, there is one advantage to these classes: your mummy-gang!

The beauty of the mummy-gang is the camaraderie, the coffee, getting your boob out in Starbucks and making genuine friends who are going through the same stages with their babies as you. My own antenatal class was a hilarious mix of people, ranging from girls who thought a natural labour involved colourless nail varnish at the pre-Caesarean pedicure, to those who are still making their own yoghurt.

At times when no one else knows how tired/bored/fat/elated/old/insane/delighted you feel, your mummy-gang from antenatal classes just get it because they're going through exactly the same thing. And chances are, your closest friends are not on maternity leave at the same time as you – you've got to hang around with someone to while away the hours until bathtime, right? But seriously, the antenatal gang is a godsend for many of us.

Yet while your crowd of new friends can be a great support, they can also be the cause of over-stressing. People don't genuinely mean to, but the competitive-mum lobe is naturally fired up. Mummies can't help but proclaim about first crawls, first teeth, first full-night's sleep (that's a *massive* one). And while they're joyously announcing this, with blow-by-blow details, everyone else is quietly neurosing, 'Yikes, mine isn't doing that ...'.

And so, unwittingly, at some points, your mummy-gang, while being fabulous in many respects, can actually become a source of anguish. Now, I'm not being dramatic – I see this weekly in my GP practice. It is very normal for a mum to come to see me to discuss something her baby *isn't* doing in comparison to his antenatal buddies. And, understandably, it causes a lot of upset. Usually, unnecessary upset.

No one means for this to happen, but it is perfectly natural for everyone to start measuring up to see whose bubba is crawling and whose is already quoting Shakespeare. And the ones left 'behind' start to feel a bit anxious. I've been there, done it and bought the *Yeah, your baby's quicker than mine* T-shirt.

The best lesson I got in dealing with competitive mummies was from my daughter whose own unique (*but completely normal*) developmental pathway meant I got caught out by the 'my baby's better than yours' chat. She sat beautifully (can you sit beautifully?) at six months, and then didn't get off her backside to cross the room until she was ready at 13 months. Thirteen months! Thirteen months: not a crawl, not a coast, not a commando. Not even a roll really. I don't even know if she ever rolled to be honest – we were waiting for the massive moment and I think I unwittingly missed it, as I got fed up of waiting.

So waiting for her to crawl became just that: a wait. With many babies crawling at nine months and plenty walking at around a year, we were certainly out on a limb. It made sitting in cafes joyous, with her perched on my lap not wanting to go anywhere. But the competitive mums, who are never merely interested in their own little love, but always interested in yours as well, couldn't help but probe:

'What does she do?'

'She sits.'

'She's 11 months. She doesn't crawl?'

'Nope.'

'Does she move on her botty?'

'No. Like I said, she just sits.'

'It's because you don't take her to Baby Tumblers,' one mum said to me.

And there was the cue for the super-duper uber-neurosis to kick in. It could actually be my fault she wasn't keeping up with baby Jones?

While her dad viewed this as a superior development pathway because we hadn't had to baby-proof the precious DVD player yet, I was of course panicking. I knew in my sensible head she was babbling and holding things as she should and generally developing well in all areas. And I also knew as a doctor that many babies don't crawl at all, and walking may not happen in a normal child until 18 months even. Both grandmas were convinced she was completely normal and clearly Oxbridge-material already, but I couldn't help but worry, mostly fuelled only by another mummy's opinion.

So I worried and waited, and worried and waited. And what happened? She bottom-shuffled at 13 months, walked at 14 months and, as her dad likes to remind me, I spent the next year moaning about how much easier my life was with a sedentary baby who didn't want to kami-kaze down the stairs. But I learnt a very important lesson early on in avoiding overly competitive mums who, if you let them, can undermine your own instinct. And that has stood me well for everything since.

So *please*, go easy on yourself with all the comparisons. Take it all with a pinch of salt. Be strong: if you feel your baby is fine and right, don't worry what other mummies think or say. Forget comparing and allow the competition to wash over you.

I know, I know, very easy for me to say, and very hard to do in reality when you're tired, new to all this baby-lark and feeling a bit vulnerable. Just remember:

- Trust your instinct: you will know if something is not right
- Concentrate on what your bubba is doing, no one else's
- Listen to the only expert that matters: YOU

Always remember what your instinct is telling you and keep calm. Before you heard about your mate's baby, had you any worries in the slightest about your baby's milestones? I bet you didn't. Try to focus on that. You and Dad think she's normal. Grandma thinks she's super-baby extraordinaire. Forget about what the other babies are doing.

Dare I say, there's also a little bit of exaggeration from some mummies about what their babies can do (you know the sort), so be mindful of that too when you're listening to all these so-called achievements. Boasting sometimes equals hot air in my experience, so I wouldn't take it too seriously. I've heard many a boastful mum rave on about her baby who slept through the night at six weeks, only for it to turn out that 'a night' actually meant 1am to 6am. Pretender!

If you can learn to overlook the comparisons now, it is great preparation for dealing with show-offy mums later when they're sizing up your child's potty-training or ballet skills. It will prepare you for those torturous moments at the school gates when a mother will insist her child begged to 'learn the harp as he just found the violin far too easy'.

Watching your baby grow and develop should be a source of delight and pride. Hanging out with other mums should be a source of laughter and support. If it isn't, you may have to find new friends.

Keep calm and heed my warning to go easy on yourself. I have seen the calmest women turn neurotic from one coffee morning with an overly competitive mum. I've even had mums in my clinic crying, after a throwaway competitive comment from another mum. So trust those instincts and listen to yourself, rather than worrying what all your baby's peers are up to.

The blame game

These are genuine comments from mums in my GP clinic:

- 'Josh isn't crawling. I know he's only seven months old, but lots of his baby friends of the same age are.'
- 'I know it's my fault he doesn't roll because we don't do baby gym.'
- 'I didn't even know about tummy time. Is that why she can't stand yet?'

Mummies and daddies are all-powerful, we are the centre of our child's world and, of course, every single thing we do for them is fundamental and crucial. But the fact of the matter is, you cannot significantly alter the age at which your baby is going to walk or recognise Chopin.

As a rational human being, before that pregnancy test pinged positive, you knew this and would never have been convinced otherwise. When sense has gone out of the window and you're faced with someone else's baby who's already doing the limbo aged 10 months, it's completely normal to get in a panic and question yourself and your parenting proficiency. I know that feeling well and I have seen it a thousand times with my patients: you know that it doesn't really matter what the other babies are doing, but then there's this gnawing little voice inside that boils up a reaction you can't even rationalise, and you start to panic because your baby isn't rolling over.

Part of this is a concern about your baby being normal. But a *massive* part of feeling this way is fuelled by guilt, just in case she's not up to speed because of you or something you've done.

There is absolutely no reason to feel guilty if your baby is not waving when some of her baby friends of the same age are. A large part of this guilt is ingrained in you from marketing of baby toys and baby classes.

Spend £99.99 on this piece of red plastic – it will enhance your child's social skills, fine motor skills and command of ancient Greek

Come to Baby Tango and improve your baby's motor and socialisation skills

Really? I mean such toys are good stimulation and a good distraction when you need a quick solo loo visit, but I think their claims are far-reaching and, dare I say, slightly overstated. Baby gym classes are lots of fun – they're sociable and a good way to kill an hour when otherwise it would be embarrassing to be in John Lewis *again*. But if you don't go, your little one is not going to have stunted development. You know this. Your instinct tells you this. It's only the advert and a few crazy mothers that tell you otherwise.

And, likewise, if you go to these classes or buy all-singing-all-dancing toys, I don't believe anyone has proven it significantly improves development. Ask yourself, if your baby claps at 11 months rather than 10 months does it make a difference? It really doesn't. The classes are fun but they are not an essential ingredient of successful parenting. You are the essential ingredient of successful parenting, not some over-priced hunk of plastic.

To test my theory, ask your mum what stimulating toys you had when you were a child or what baby classes you went to. (Prepare for her to laugh at you.) Most of us grew up eating grass and watching our parents do the washing-up. Apparently, I spent a lot of time sitting in cardboard boxes (conclude from that what you will). But the truth is all this paraphernalia and the myriad of stimulation-enhancing toys didn't exist, it wasn't part of the parenting agenda and we all developed fine. We crawled, we ran, we clapped without the over-priced kit and scheduled programme. In the generations before ours, parents were far too time-pressed to worry about the minutiae of baby's timetable.

Likewise, children developed normally 500 years ago. And likewise children do in parts of the world where poverty prevails and where socialising and stimulating playtime are the last things on anyone's minds.

Here is an exhaustive list of what babies need to develop normally:

- Love
- Food

- Sleep
- Warmth
- Some more love

That is all. Of course I'm not suggesting your babies don't need toys or fun or that you should cancel baby music classes and throw her playthings away. I'm not in any way suggesting you shouldn't do what you think is the best for your baby, of course you should. These things are fun for you and fun for baby. They're part of parenting nowadays and the fabric of bringing up babies in the 21st century, in the developed world. I'm just urging a bit of realism, and a bit of chilling out about what stimulation babies need, and what if anything is achieved by it.

When you are feeling a bit loopy or stressed about your baby's social diary and unique talents versus baby Moonbeam down the road, have a think about families with four and five children: I have plenty of patients with four children. (Incidentally, four is the new three apparently.) Mums with four kids do not have time to schlep the smallest one to baby Zumba classes because there are far more pressing things on the horizon to do for the older ones. A fabulous friend of mine had twins from her third pregnancy: when they were a year old, we were talking about baby classes. 'Baby classes?' she sneered. 'They don't even go out of the house!' And fourth children roll, crawl, walk, talk and do everything they're supposed to, even without the pressure to perform heaped on first-borns! My second child wasn't subjected to all the activity classes number one did, but rather spent a lot of time sitting in my wardrobe playing with my shoes. And he developed just fine.

Babies need whatever stimulation you can give them: nothing more, nothing less. You are not failing if you opt out of these activities (you won't even contemplate them with your third baby, believe me). Likewise you have certainly not failed if she crawls/waves/walks/talks after the other babies.

- Your baby's development will follow her own unique pathway
- Classes and toys are fun, not essential
- Feeling guilty about her development is not an option

Developmental stages and ages that are important

This is not a guide to memorise or stick on the fridge. There are no prizes for meeting these milestones early. This is definitely not an absolute list, but simply a few pointers I think parents could find helpful. There are plenty of definitive lists available and you should find a record of developmental stages in your baby's red personal health record book.

As with everything else we have talked about with your baby, there are vast swathes of opinion and pseudo-expertise about development and what babies should be doing and when. When should your baby recite Homer from memory? At what age should your baby do a cart-wheel? But buried beneath all the nonsense and drivel that is spoken on the subject, there are actually a few genuinely important guidelines regarding development. Don't worry, just a few that you need to recognise. Even if these weren't written here, you'd notice them without thinking about it.

There are milestones in the first year that your baby should reach at some point to reassure you that she is on track. There aren't many, but they are significant. They tell you what you know already: that your baby is okay and is thriving and flourishing.

In the UK we don't pro-actively or routinely check up on healthy babies. I like this. We don't offer monthly or yearly paediatrician check-ups – we wait for you to tell us if something concerns you, rather than looking for problems. Us doctors acknowledge wholeheartedly that mums know best, and if there's a problem you'll tell us. We don't need to offer you regular MOTs because we trust you and your instinct. I stand by the fact that mummies instinctively know if their babies are developing at the correct rate. You just *know*. How? I don't know but you know. Like everything else, the maternal instinct is there – you just have to listen to the instinct, rather than all the codswallop around. Remember, you are the expert as far as your baby is concerned.

The developmental tables I have given below are a guide to empower your instinct and help you decide if something may or may not be wrong. Please, please, please remember that developmental stages are not exact ages but a spectrum. This is really crucial. For example, the average age of walking is one year, but normal can be anything from nine months to 18 months. So much of the so-called lateness isn't really late, it's just one end of normal. View it as one end of a spectrum rather than a 'delay'. Only once you get to a certain late-point or limit, should you seek advice. At any time, if you feel something (whatever that may be) is not right, you should see your health visitor.

- Trust your instinct
- Keep calm and listen to yourself

There are four areas of development and in the first year a huge amount goes on. Parents tend to focus on the big ones, such as walking, but the others are equally important. When doctors like me assess babies for development, we look at every aspect to get the full picture: we call this looking at the child 'globally'. Each area of development is crucial, not just the headline ones, such as walking and talking. It's vital to remember this: I find when parents are concerned about an unmet milestone, they tend to ignore all the stuff their baby *can* do, and focus on the one thing she can't.

1. **Big movement skills:** Known as gross motor skills, big movements are what everyone notices – this is what grannies comment on, and daddies boast about. I tend to find this is what parents concentrate on the most. The big ones:

	Baby-average will do this at ...	When you're allowed to worry ...	And by the way ...
Head control	6 weeks	If your baby is not doing this at 8 weeks.	This should have been checked at your 6–8 week appointment with your GP.
Sitting	6 months, but will still be unsteady.	If he's not sitting well at 8 months.	Sitting is very important as it shows your baby has developed normal reflexes.
Walking	12 months	18 months for a chat with the GP, but this is still one end of normal.	Bottom-shufflers tend to walk later than crawlers.

Babies will do some sort of pre-walking movement often before they are a year old – crawling, bottom-shuffling and, my own personal favourite, 'commando crawling', which makes them look like mini-Marines. It isn't helpful in my opinion to label when babies should be doing their chosen pre-walking style: as I've shown you with my own offspring, you can't actually quantify these ones and they don't particularly tell you very much. There is such an enormous difference between babies. Making a comparison here is merely stress-inducing with little benefit!

Don't forget that thanks to the lifesaving cot-death guidelines, we know we have fewer crawlers than we used to. Since all babies now sleep on their backs to prevent cot death, they're less used to being on their tummies and so fewer babies are crawling and more are bottom-shuffling.

This is absolutely nothing to worry about. A baby does not need to crawl to develop normally.

The notion of *tummy time* was invented to give babies some time on their tummy. It is definitely not complicated and simply involves letting her try out lying on her tummy while playing each day. Some babies really only like this for a minute or two before protesting. Others absolutely love it and it becomes their preferred playing position. Once they're rolling around and then sitting up it becomes irrelevant, as she'll position herself just the way she wants to be.

2. **Little movement skills:** Known as fine motor skills, the little movements are actually far more interesting than the big stuff, and pretty fundamental as they are closely tied in with being able to see properly. I see far fewer fears from parents about these skills than the others, but they are significant. Some for you to notice:

	Baby-average will do this at …	When you're allowed to worry …	And by the way …
Following a moving object by moving her head.	6 weeks	If your baby is not doing this at 10 weeks.	This is a really important test of vision.
Passing a block from one hand to the other.	6 months	8 months	She's probably doing this all the time, and no one's noticed!

Pincer grip	10 months	12 months	This means your baby being able to hold something small, such as a raisin, between her thumb and finger.

Pointing is another favourite of mine – babies start to point with their index finger at about 10–12 months old and this is a recognised developmental stage. It is also the first in a long list of ways they can embarrass their parents.

3. **Baby talk:** If, when and what babies can say is legitimately important as an indicator of their development and also as a marker of their hearing. It's possibly the one time when you should be comparing your baby to her peers, to check she's up to speed with things. Babies born in the UK undergo a newborn hearing test, but normal speech development is a crucial way to detect hearing problems that may have been missed or that have subsequently developed.

	Baby-average will do this at ...	When you're allowed to worry ...	And by the way ...
Make 'Oooo, aaaa, eee' cooing (vowel noises)	4 months	6 months	A lot of babies do this from as early as 10 weeks.

| Ma, da, ba talk | 6 months | 10 months | Don't expect Daddy to be said to the right person until later. |
| 3–5 words, usually including mama and dada. | 12 months | 14 months is a good time to have a chat with the GP. | Variants of drink, milk and bottle are common ones. |

First words cause much joy, hilarity and pride and rightly so, but they are also genuinely significant so listen carefully. Even if your newborn has passed the hearing test, she can subsequently develop hearing issues such as glue ear, which may hinder her first words. It's an important thing to look out for as often delayed speech is your only clue.

4. **Social skills:** These are another great source of mummy-pride: I never have a one-year-old leave my surgery without mum saying, 'Wave bye-bye to Dr Cannon.' Seeing your baby as a social creature is magnificent, with that first smile being one of the seminal moments of parenthood – even if it was just wind really.

	Baby-average will do this at …	When you're allowed to worry …	And by the way …
Non-windy smile (at you if you're lucky).	6 weeks	8 weeks	This should have been checked at your 6-week appointment.

| Separation anxiety and fear of strangers. | 8 months | Some babies don't notice mum leaving the room ever – while it may upset you, it is no cause for concern. | It is normal for babies to go from liking strangers to shyness around the age of 9 months. |
| Waves bye-bye | 10 months | 12 months | If you're lucky, you'll get a kiss too. |

How your baby feeds herself also contributes to the social milestones, but there are huge variations here depending on a lot of factors: for example, how she weaned or which sippy cup you used. If you gave her finger food early on, it makes sense that she's going to be better at popping food into her mouth with a good aim, than her best mate who's still being fed from a spoon by mummy. Even breastfeeding will affect this: a lot of one-year-olds will drink from a cup, *but* if your baby is still having the majority of her drinks from the boob at aged one (perfectly normal), it's obviously going to take her slightly longer to get used to a sippy cup.

What to do if you are worried

If you are genuinely troubled that your baby hasn't met a milestone or something seems not right, don't hesitate to seek advice from your GP. It can be reassuring to ask friends (the non-competitive ones) and your own mum, but often you just need that objective, experienced opinion for ultimate reassurance. There is nothing at all wrong with that. Highlighting a concern to the GP early doesn't make you overly neurotic; it makes you sensible. Problems can be easier to solve the earlier they're detected; with speech, for example. Keep calm, trust your instinct and do what you feel is right. A good GP will never make you feel embarrassed for being concerned. If you are worried about something, developmental or otherwise, it is important to get a decent medical opinion from a GP or a paediatrician.

- Keep calm
- Trust your instinct
- Listen to the baby expert: YOU

Chapter 9

When Your Baby is Ill – What You Need to Know

We live in a funny world where we offer parenting classes to teach new mums and dads how to deliver a placenta, but not what to do when their baby is ill. It is, quite frankly, astounding that most parents have been instructed about baby massage, but not what constitutes a fever. So if your baby is ill and you're feeling rather poorly equipped, you're in good company! Parents aren't taught this stuff – it won't have featured in your antenatal classes, so you'll end up learning most of it as you're going along. It's a trial and error situation, at possibly the worst time for a trial and error situation.

Out of all the aspects of babyhood, this was one of the main reasons I felt compelled to write this book. I found year after year that many mums didn't know the basics of looking after a poorly baby and realised that the parenting arena had got its priorities wrong. You're bombarded with loads and loads of information you don't need, but not the essential stuff you do. So for sensible, down-to-earth mummies I wanted to redress that balance.

In a book where I have prided myself on dictating no rules, some rules have sneaked in here. These are actually the few, vital rules I wish all new parents did know. These are the ones that are worth listening to; guidelines that come from genuine experts like paediatricians. So indulge me in a bit of rule-giving and finger-wagging just for this chapter.

Knowing what to do when your baby is poorly is crucial for all empowered parents. It's a time when even the calmest of people lose their cool: it's uber-stressful, upsetting and, quite frankly, often scary. Understanding a few basics really helps your baby and you.

When my baby had her first cold aged three months, I remember just sitting watching her all day to see what was going to happen. She wasn't even that unwell, just a bit watery-eyed and snotty. But I just felt I needed to literally keep an eye on her; I even called my mum over to take shifts with me watching the snot.

'What are we watching for?' she asked.

'No idea.'

'So why are we doing it?'

'No idea.'

'Can I read the paper?'

'No, just watch the baby.'

Well, that was a fun-filled day as you can imagine. I'm in no way suggesting you do that, because it was unnecessary; the point is, it's very normal to feel like you don't know what you're doing when your baby gets his first cold or cough. I'm a doctor, and I even felt a bit out of my depth.

But there are some basics that you should know that

will stand you in good stead for whenever your baby is ill, whether he's aged three months, three years or 13.

The basics of looking after your baby when he's poorly go back to the fundamentals that I believe underlie everything. You must trust yourself, trust your instinct and be guided by your baby. Mums know when their babies are not well and you must always listen to yourself. I learnt very early on in my paediatric training that maternal instinct is never to be ignored – a notion I have seen proved right over and over again. At this point YOU know best.

- Trust your instinct
- Keep calm
- If you feel panicked, consult your GP

Why babies get ill

It is natural and common for babies to get minor illnesses in their first year. They are little, they've never come across all the germs before and their immune systems need to learn to cope with all the nasties that are flying around. Unless you are choosing to bring up your baby in a hermetically sealed isolated commune (please don't), he will be vulnerable to infections. This is standard and all babies go through the usual catalogue of coughs, colds, snots, fevers, vomits and diarrhoea episodes.

Some babies seem to get more infections than others. This is simply a spectrum of normal: the same way some babies will walk at 11 months and others at 18 months.

Thankfully we are not all the same: all babies are different. Part of that is the environment they're brought up in, but part of it is just them. Winter babies, babies in nursery, social-butterfly babies will possibly get more infections than others, but that's completely expected.

I am often asked by mummies if it is normal for their baby to get minor illnesses so often. This is not an easy question to answer, and really it takes a proper consultation with a doctor to decide. If a baby is in nursery, I would say one cold or virus a month is pretty much normal: annoying (especially as you can't get a refund) but true. The clues to look for that this is fine are:

- He recovers easily from them.
- He's well in between.
- He's feeding, growing and developing normally.
- He's just getting bog-standard snotty-type illnesses.
- Instinct tells you he is fine.

A word about guilt. Guilt seems to creep its mean way into every aspect of this motherhood-lark, doesn't it? Far too often I've heard a mum suggest her baby got a cold because she took him to the park or to a music class: 'It's my fault because he goes to nursery' type comments. Please, please, please don't even entertain these thoughts. Going out, socialising, seeing other humans is a normal, important part of your life and your baby's life and getting little viruses or a bit of cough is a perfectly normal consequence of that.

You are not supposed to keep your baby wrapped up at home, with no fresh air and no human contact so he doesn't get ill. You must not feel guilty or responsible if you get a cold, then your baby gets it. Evolution has thankfully sorted this out for us: our babies can cope with this. They are not built to live in isolation: immune systems are designed to help our bodies fight infection, but they only learn to fight infection if they are exposed to it. Whether that is at home from a dad with man-flu, or whether that's in the supermarket or a baby music class. Your baby is going to come into contact with germs and, quite frankly, needs to for his immune system to develop.

Now, clearly I'm not suggesting the pair of you spend every day in the doctor's waiting room waving viruses into his nostrils. Just keep things in perspective. It is nobody's fault when your baby gets a cold or tummy upset. It is a natural part of life, and if you want a positive spin on it, a regular way for an immune system to develop. So while I know it is unlikely you will be congratulating yourself when your baby gets the snots, go easy on yourself. It's life.

Seeing your GP

The chances are by the time your baby is a year old, he will have had at least one snot-fest, probably one cough-type illness or one rash. Your GP will become someone who has gone from that faceless bloke you saw once a year for your Pill check, to a cherished friend you speak to more than your own sister. This is why I've ended up friends with many mummy-patients: because we have such regular conversations. And that is fine. That is standard and us doctors expect to see you when your baby is unwell. It is never wrong to go to the doctor because you are concerned about your baby. No good GP will ever make you feel like a time-waster if your baby is not himself. This is all new to you and if you need that bit of reassurance to empower your own mummy-skills it is no problem, and not wrong. If you think your baby is just 'not right' a trip to the GP, even if you are reassured and sent home, is never a waste of time.

Yes, there are better ways to spend a morning than sitting in a germ-filled waiting room, but it is never a mistake to take a little one to the doctor. If you find you're made to feel uncomfortable for seeking help, it could be time to find a new GP.

What is and isn't important when your baby is poorly

I have included this list, and gone into more detail below, because these are the things mums notice and tell me about when their baby is unwell. Mummies don't always know which ones to worry about and which to ignore. This is not a definitive list of every sign that a baby could be unwell – just the things I know will concern you:

What is important when your baby is unwell:	What is less important:
Fever	Loss of appetite for solids
Any rash	Snot colour

What is important when your baby is unwell:	What is less important:
Playing/alertness	The exact number on the thermometer
Fluids in and out	Being tired
Vomiting	

My baby is hot

Within the first year of his life, your baby will almost certainly have a fever at some point. Common causes of this would be a cough or a cold, a tummy upset or a viral illness. Obviously there are also more serious concerns such as ear infections, urine infections and chest infections.

The best way to tell if a baby has a fever is by touching his skin. This is cheap, accurate and readily available at all times. Thermometers are the second best way simply because you can get too focused on the numbers, rather than the baby. While medically, we define a fever as being 38°C or above, the severity of the illness is not dependent on the number alone. You see, I've seen children with temperatures of 38°C who are floppy, dehydrated and need admission to hospital. But I've also seen kids run into my clinic eating biscuits and causing complete mayhem, and when I take their temperature it's 39.5°C. And yes, I do have an accurate thermometer. The number is not the whole story. The whole story comes from looking at the whole child: for example, feeding, happiness rating, activity levels. Not just the figure. I always tell my patients 'look at the baby not the temperature'.

The best way really to tell if your baby has a fever is to feel his skin yourself. If he feels hot and looks red, if his forehead, chest or back feels hot, that is a good way to tell. Trust yourself to know if your baby has a fever. You are used to touching him and you'll easily spot the difference.

Lots of doctor-parents I know don't own thermometers for their kids. They rely on the good old-fashioned hand on skin method, because it works. Plenty of my patients can't afford to buy a good thermometer and they learn very quickly how to tell if their baby is hot. It's certainly not essential. I do have a thermometer at home. It's used far more often to take teddies' temperatures than for any children.

If you do use a thermometer, a figure above 38 degrees constitutes a fever. Sometimes I meet mums who come in with a graph on their Smart phone of the temperature throughout the day: it isn't necessary because it's far more important to look at the baby, not a bar chart.

Here comes a rule, a genuine one: all children aged under six months with a fever, either measured on a thermometer or by your hand, should go to the GP for a consult. For a baby aged over six months, be guided by how you feel your baby is, and if you have any doubts head down to the GP.

Coping with the fevers your baby has will become second nature to you but in the beginning it will stress you out. Err on the side of caution as far as going to the GP. You can safely bring a temperature down with medicine such as children's paracetamol or ibuprofen suspension: both of these drugs reduce fever and ease pain in babies.

As long as you use the correct dosing, using infant paracetamol or ibuprofen is perfectly appropriate if your baby is in pain or has a fever. Your pharmacist can guide you as to which ones are the best and the different tastes: very important with children's medicine. Whether you use a spoon or a syringe depends on your baby, and what he will take. For genuine medicine haters, your GP can prescribe paracetamol suppositories, which are a sneaky but effective way of getting medicine in when necessary. Medicine is not always necessary: don't ignore other non-medical ways that can help too like keeping your baby in cooler clothing and dabbing him with a damp flannel. You can also gently cool down a room to cool down a baby. Do this by opening a window slightly or putting a fan on at the other side of a room to where you and baby are.

Hydration, hydration, hydration

No matter whether your baby simply has a cold or anything that involves a temperature, drinking is the most crucial thing. It takes hours, not days, for babies to get dehydrated. Having a fever, vomiting or having diarrhoea uses up water and that all needs to be replaced.

For babies who still only drink milk, giving the milk and cooled, boiled water is essential to rehydrate. If your baby is already weaned and drinking diluted juice as well as milk, offer that. Let him have whatever drink he wants. Now is not the time to be fussing over the rules of what babies should drink. Of course I don't want you to give your baby lemonade, but if you know he always drinks more if he has diluted apple juice, go with that to ensure he's hydrated. At this stage getting the fluid in is critical. Buying rehydration salts is not necessary unless a doctor says so: they don't taste great and water does the same thing.

Often, babies will drink less when they are poorly and it is important to watch that. In the panic of a baby being unwell, it can get a bit fraught so here's my *keep calm* advice: work out how much your baby normally drinks and halve it. This is the absolute minimum he should be taking in and is your own unique guide. It doesn't matter if this is usually milk, but it's now all water as long as the fluid is going in. If he drops below your 50 per cent level, you must seek medical advice.

If you are breastfeeding, you'll be guided by your boobs. If they're starting to feel too full, your baby may not be taking enough milk. Make sure you are also drinking enough so your milk supply is at its best. And offer your baby cooled, boiled water as well to top-up.

The best way to tell if a baby is hydrated is checking that he is weeing. Gauge this on the number of wet nappies he normally has and if it is around the same or a bit less then he's fine. Sometimes you can't tell if there's a wee, thanks to today's super-duper dry-as-a-bone nappies or because the nappy is also full of poo. If that's the case, pop a cotton wool ball into the front of the nappy – if he pees, the ball will get wet, it's super-easy to see. If your baby has dry nappies for more than half a day, it indicates dehydration so see your GP. Having dry lips, a dry mouth and no tears are also signs of dehydration, but these are all just pointers – if your instinct tells you your baby is dehydrated, never mind the rigid signs, listen to yourself and seek help.

Now here is some foolish advice parents are given, that I object to: 'To see if your baby is dehydrated, have a feel of the soft spot (fontanelle) on their head and see if it is sunken.' Indeed this is very true, and this is one of the signs doctors look for. But this is downright crazy advice to give parents – how many times have you felt your baby's soft spot on a good day? Probably, never. The trouble with advising you to feel a soft spot is that, understandably, most of you have no idea what you are feeling for. Which leads to the scenario I have witnessed more than once, where a very sensible mummy has come to me with a perfectly well baby just because she wasn't sure if his head felt a bit sunken. You don't know what you are feeling for, or how sunken is 'sunken', so it leads to tremendous confusion. Fontanelles are different in all babies and change as a baby gets older Measuring soft spots is bad advice when you should be concentrating on monitoring the easy things – the fluids in and wee-wees out. Stick with that. Leave the soft spots to the doctors.

Feeding is not just about the fluids

The first thing I ask a mum when she brings in her unwell baby is whether the baby is drinking his bottle or breast-feeding. This is not just about hydration. If a baby has a temperature or any little illness, but can still take a good breastfeed or the majority of his bottle, it tells you so much about him. It tells you he's alert, he's got energy, he's interested and is unlikely to get dehydrated. Taking full milk feeds is reassuring when a baby is unwell. Drinking milk is hard work for a baby, particularly a baby under three months old, so if he can do that it shows he has energy and is not too unwell. A good sign for mummies I reckon. (That is also why I say playing is important: if your baby can be bothered to play, it shows he is alert and has energy; if he is floppy, weak and not interested in playing, that is a worry.)

If a baby is in the middle of a snot-fest or a cough, it can be hard work to finish a feed in one go. You may find you have to start and stop particularly if he has a blocked nose. Now is not the time to be worrying about feeding times and exact schedules: just remember your 50 per cent guide (see page 162). If ensuring he's drinking enough means you're feeding on and off throughout the day, then so be it. For now, that's how it is. Any schedule or routine you had before will ping back once he's back to normal. Illness is definitely a time for a go-with-the-flow mentality as far as schedules and times are concerned. Even if you have decided to be a very strictly routine mamma, let loose to ensure he gets enough feeds into him and all the rest he needs.

If your baby is struggling or uninterested in his milk, then that is a clear sign to go to the GP. This can happen because he's congested and snotty, but can also be a sign that he's weak or working hard to breathe.

Rashes

I could list for you all the rashes I see in babies under one and it would be an entire book of its own. If your baby is unwell, particularly if he is hot, a rash serves not as a signal for you to try and diagnose it, but simply for you to head to the doctor. We don't expect you to tell the difference between roseola and heat rash. That's our job. A rash is simply a cue for you to seek help.

A rash is, thankfully, very rarely a reason to panic, but it is worth the reassurance of a proper diagnosis. Rashes scare parents and that's completely understandable because of the fear of meningitis. Babies often get faint rashes when they have a fever, and it is no cause for concern.

This is worth sticking on the fridge:

> ***The rash of meningitis does NOT disappear when you press it with a glass. This is a 999 call.***

I find that, in a state of panic, parents forget if the meningitis rash is supposed to stay or go, so write it down somewhere. Even young babies get meningitis and even vaccinated babies get meningitis. Never wait on this one.

He won't eat

Us mummies, we just love our babies to eat. Once they're on to solids and enjoying all that green mush or hand-squidged toast, there's nothing more satisfying than seeing them filling their little tummies. Which is why it's so disappointing when they stop!

No matter how unwell babies are, even with the most minor of colds, they don't eat their solids. All that lovely broccoli purée and teddy-shaped pasta wasted. It's very sad, but babies lose their appetite for solids when they are unwell. This shouldn't alarm you or concern you. It is a sign something is amiss, but it is no more sinister than that. It is certainly not a sign they are desperately unwell, as loss of appetitie happens even with the mildest of colds.

Not eating worries us parents a lot, but it shouldn't: in the context of a cough or a cold or a tummy upset it is par for the course. And more often than not, your baby's appetite will recover a few days after he has. That too is normal – it seems to take time for it to catch up. Just be patient. Your baby is not going to lose those beautiful fat bracelets by not eating properly for a few days. Still offer your baby food as normal, perhaps just his favourite. If he only eats carrots or yoghurt every day for a few days, it doesn't really matter while he's unwell. Any schedule or meal plan will be back on track once he's better. Be guided by what he seems to want, and never force him to eat. It's the drinking that counts (see page 161), not the food.

Snot, snot and more snot

I talk about snot a lot. Probably more than I talk about poo. Snot, mucus, phlegm, bogies: whatever you want to call it. You have never seen so much snot as when you become a parent. Snot is as normal a part of parenting as nappies or milk or arguing with your other half over who's more tired (it's never him).

Babies get snotty a lot: the quantity of snot will astound you, the colour of it will amaze you and, yes, the frequency will frustrate you. The reason it's pretty damn annoying is because there's little you can do about it. It's very reassuring to be told, don't worry it's just a cold, but actually that leaves you with a miserable baby who genuinely looks like he's got the lurgy, and even his doting grandma is a bit horrified.

Let me bust a well-known snot-myth: green snot does not mean your baby needs an antibiotic. This is an urban myth that is not true. Green snot just means he has, well, green snot. It's probably an infection, yes, but is most likely to be a virus that needs no special treatment.

While snot is not a significant sign in itself, it can lead to your baby having difficulty drinking because he's so congested. That's why it's important to have some snot-busting ideas. Here's a realistic action plan for snot-filled days and nights:

- **Use snot-suckers:** I hated these but I have to admit the majority of my patients swear by them and positively gloat about removing all that gloop.

- **Humidify his room:** Do this cheaply with a wet towel on a warm radiator. Or you can buy a humidifier. Moistening the air makes snot looser and easier to dribble away.

- **Tilt the cot slightly:** If your baby sleeps ever so slightly upright, snot can dribble out his nose to clear his airways.

- **Feed little and often:** Congestion can stop your baby taking a good feed in one swoop.

- **Use baby vapour rubs:** These can help loosen hard congested mucus from your baby's little nose.

As yet we have no medicine you can give babies that miraculously gets rid of this gunk. Believe me, if we did, I'd buy shares in the stuff. Snot invariably lasts a week or two, and as long as your baby is drinking and you've got plenty of tissues in the house, you don't need to panic. And, no, I don't care if it's green.

Sleepy or drowsy?

There is an essential difference between being tired, which is fine for a poorly baby, and being drowsy, which is not fine. Babies will be more tired when they are ill: think of yourself when you have flu. You need to sleep more in the day and the night and still have no energy even to turn the telly on. That is how us humans recover from things. We need to sleep.

So it is very normal to see babies having longer naps or more naps or a longer night's sleep when they are under the weather. That is fine and you must let your baby do that. Routine or no routine, sleep is important when you are ill and the schedule doesn't matter: it will soon ping back into place once your baby has recovered. The more he sleeps, the sooner and easier he'll recover. We expect babies to sleep more when they are ill, even with a minor cold.

Being drowsy is different from being tired. Drowsiness is when you can't wake your baby easily, or he seems constantly asleep, or much less alert, and not interested in feeding or waking for feeds. Drowsiness is not normal, and is always a reason to see the doctor urgently.

The illness with no name – a virus

A really good friend of mine has banned me from using the word virus with her. She said after three kids she is fed up hearing that word. Every time she goes to the GP with some cough/sore throat/snot extravaganza that is what she is told: 'It's just a virus.' She says, 'Why can't these things have names? It's always just a virus – isn't that a cop-out?'

It's not actually a cop-out. Most of the minor illnesses our babies get are, thankfully, just viruses and that is great. To be honest, when you go to the GP you do want to be told, 'It's just a virus.' Viruses are the simple infections your baby, and you, will get that resolve easily and need no antibiotics. Of course there are some serious viruses, but in the context of snot-fests and little coughs, a virus is what you want. Sure, there's no specific treatment, but they get better easily and are generally not serious.

Viruses do not need to be treated with antibiotics, which is fantastic as it is always better to avoid yucky medicines and their possible side-effects. I know many people think antibiotics are a quick fix but the reality is they're not unless there genuinely is a bacterial infection.

You're doing the healthy bacteria in your baby's guts a favour if you can avoid them.

It should be reassuring when you're told it's just a simple, boring virus with no name. You don't want anything with a more interesting name than that.

It's still all about the instinct

No matter how many rules and pointers I have just described, when your baby is unwell you have to let your instinct thrive and guide you. Mummies know when something is 'up'. That's true when their child is a few hours old, and it's true when they're 18 years old.

Often you can't say exactly why your baby seems unwell. There may be none of the signs I've listed in this chapter: just your gut feeling. There's no number on the thermometer, no specific rash, no checklist criteria ticked off. It's just something about your baby: the way he looks, the way he feels, the way he smells, even. It's often something you can feel and no one else. Plenty of times I have mummies tell me:

- 'I could just tell he wasn't right.'
- 'He just doesn't seem himself.'
- 'Something's not right.'

You can't be taught that, it's just there in you. It's a reflex and it's important. As important as any rash, or any fever. It's not always tangible, but if you feel something isn't right then go with that and seek help. Even when your baby is unwell, you are still the parenting expert.

- Keep calm
- Trust your instinct
- Listen to the baby expert: YOU

Chapter 10
Vaccinations – A Rule Dr Ellie Appreciates!

Within the first few weeks after birth, you will be invited to vaccinate your baby at the local baby clinic. Probably not the coolest invitation your little one will ever receive, but actually the most valuable. Buried beneath the messy swamp of guidelines, pseudo-expertise and dogma you will have to navigate, finally here is something that really matters! Actually, it is one of the most vital 'rules' you will face as a new parent.

However, although I believe vaccinations are imperative, I want you as a super-duper parenting-expert extraordinaire to make your own mind up. Vaccination guidelines are evidence-based science developed over years by doctors and public health gurus. But you should still ponder and consider them for yourself. I'm not suggesting you whip out the petri dishes and play with blobs of bacteria (my scientific training didn't extend to the proper term for 'blob'). What I mean is that YOU must be 100 per cent at ease with all the decisions you make for your baby. This means understanding the reason we vaccinate so you can make an informed choice for your baby.

I wish there wasn't an anti-vaccination 'gang' but there is. If you've not already come across them, I'm surprised. They're normally lurking online, in mums' chatroom threads and on Facebook pages. Sadly this means a great deal of dangerous and confusing myths have been perpetuated about vaccinations. As someone in the business of saving lives, this is terribly heartbreaking for me, but I'm a realist and accept it is a fact of life. And actually it's due to the myths out there that I feel even more compelled to talk about vaccinations: I don't welcome the peddling of false phoney-science, but I do welcome sensible discussions by empowered parents (that's you) wanting to do the best for their babies. Listening to yourself and trusting that all-powerful instinct is what matters here. You are making a big choice for your precious little one that will impact on her lifelong health: knowing the facts should help you make the best decision for her.

There is no conspiracy: GPs like myself aren't being paid by nasty pharmaceutical giants to jab your baby. But, equally, it is still your job to question and evaluate anything that happens to your baby, so all parents should understand all the clinical decisions that your doctor takes for you. That includes vaccination. Even if you are fervently in favour of vaccination, you should understand what you are giving your baby, and what you have protected her against.

Vaccinating babies is recommended by the World Health Organisation, the Royal College of Paediatrics, and the Department of Health (and for the sake of argument more than 100 other bona fide medical establishments around the world). But, ultimately, however clever they may be, these medical bigwigs don't matter: it is YOU who have to be at ease with your individual decision for your baby. Along with all other parenting decisions you make, YOU have to feel comfortable with your choice and live with it.

As a doctor, I genuinely consider vaccination to be one of mankind's greatest inventions, along with mascara and dishwashers of course. Seriously, if you ever get the chance to read even a brief history of medicine you will see the colossal impact vaccinations have had on public health: our kids won't ever hear of diphtheria, yet not so long ago this illness killed the child and grandchild of Queen Victoria. Nowadays, whether you live in Buckingham Palace or Buckinghamshire, you don't have this concern. Along with clean water and proper sewers (we can thank those clever Romans for that), vaccination has been responsible for saving the lives of millions of children around the globe.

I have two children and they are both fully vaccinated. One of the reasons I sleep well at night is because I know I have done all I can to protect them from fatal illnesses. Being a natural worrier, vaccinations allow me to keep calm and relax about something: the ultimate way to avoid guilt in my opinion! As a mummy I seriously believe vaccination is a gift for our kids and it's easy to forget how lucky we are to live in a country where it is available, accessible and free.

My daughter was born in the years following the MMR scandal when many of my friends and mummy-crowd contemplated and opted out of the vaccination. I'd be lying if I said I didn't think twice about it: of course I did. It was a very worrying time for parents, especially new mums with a tendency towards neurosis. As I'm sure you've realised by now, being a doctor has not particularly protected me from the anxiety and bewilderment all mummies face (my other half can certainly verify this if you need proof). But luckily for me, and for my daughter more importantly, I had the opportunity to have rational discussions with medical colleagues. And, in the end, of course I believed in the safety and benefits of the vaccinations, far more than the media-hype and the scaremongering headlines (more of that later). But crucially, it was *my* decision as a mummy – and her dad of course as well: that all-important instinct fought its way out despite all the craziness and confusion around at the time.

Just like I did, you have to make the correct decision for your baby and yourself. Just remember

- Listen to the real facts
- Trust yourself to make the right choice
- Keep calm in the face of confusing myths and junk pseudo-science

When is the last time you talked about polio?

There's so much to talk about after you've had a baby: nappies, sleep, breastfeeding, annoying husbands, sleep, nipples, annoying in-laws, formula, nannies, sleep, nurseries, perineums, sleep, snot, poo, exhaustion, reflux, sleep. Up and down the country, across cyberspace, around the globe, mums are having the same conversations about the big topics that affect us and our babies. I had these conversations when I had my first child 10 years ago; I'm having the same conversations with my patients now. I expect to have them with my kids when they have their babies. The worries and questions are pretty universal. And throughout all these chats, the funny ones, the serious ones, the neurotic ones, online, on the phone, in Starbucks (again), I bet you have never sat around discussing polio. Am I right?

Of course I am right. Why would you be talking about polio? I have never discussed polio either as a mummy or a doctor. I'm not even sure I discussed it at medical school, and I went to a pretty good one.

'Why on earth would anyone be discussing polio?', 'We don't need to worry about polio, it has disappeared hasn't it?', 'I don't even know what polio is!' And that is exactly the point. You're not chatting about polio with your antenatal posse because there's no need. No one knows what polio is any more because it is no longer important. No parent in the UK needs to worry about polio any more. The worry has been eradicated: and that is the reason we vaccinate our children.

Polio is a potentially fatal, incurable disease caused by a virus that within hours can cause a child to become irreversibly paralysed. It mainly affects children aged under five. But, thankfully, you don't need to worry about it.

Your grandparents had to worry, but you don't. Your lovely baby won't talk about it, and her children won't either. The concern and fear has been eliminated.

In the first half of the 20th century the very word *polio* would strike fear in the heart of all parents, just like the word *meningitis* does now. *Polio* was synonymous with death, cripple, pain and disability. Thousands of children were paralysed every year until the introduction of a successful vaccination in the 1950s in the UK.

As recently as 1988, 1,000 children *a day* globally were paralysed by polio. Yet 20 years later, after a gigantic worldwide vaccination effort, fewer than 2,000 cases were reported *for the entire year*. The numbers are staggering, aren't they?

A disease that was crippling thousands of children a day worldwide has been eradicated from all but three countries around the world. The risk to the children in the UK is now so tiny we've pretty much confined it to the history books. We even give a weaker vaccine now because the risk is so small it doesn't warrant the stronger one we used to administer.

The history of polio perfectly illustrates how vaccination is lifesaving. It works and saves lives, not just from death but from suffering and disability. The disease has been fought, and the human race has won. We don't ever stop to think about our children becoming lame from polio; it is not on any parenting radar any more, it isn't even on my medical radar. In the long list of parental worries these days, polio wouldn't even make the top 500. And yes, by the way, I probably could name the first 499.

Polio never comes up in any conversation I have in clinic other than when I'm explaining the vaccination schedule to a patient. This is the success of vaccinations: we can afford to forget about devastating diseases. This is why on an individual basis parents choose vaccination for their babies, and why on a global scale the World Health Organisation strives to vaccinate all children around the world.

Those who don't believe in vaccination

People do have concerns about vaccination and I acknowledge that. There is little point in the medical profession ignoring these concerns and being didactic. Doctors have done themselves no favours over the years with their God-complexes: we need to be sympathetic, not tyrannical! I'd rather address worries and help people make the safest decision than dictate guidelines that parents feel compelled to follow mindlessly. This book is all about not doing things mindlessly, but thinking for yourself and trusting your instinct.

That is why I'd like to address some of the common myths regarding vaccination, in the hope that with a sensible discussion, you as a parent can make an informed choice like I did. First of all, though, a word about folk who do not believe in or are *in opposition to* vaccination. I meet only a few in my surgery, the majority of whom are parents trying to do the best for their children and are open to a rational discussion. Those parents are making a choice and while I disagree, it is not my place as a doctor to judge, criticise or condemn. I wish their children were vaccinated, but I have to respect their decision that they're not. However, there is another much larger group of people who are not necessarily parents themselves but they form what could be described as an anti-vaccination *lobby*, and they are very interested in what you're doing for your baby. They target the good work of the world-wide medical profession by trying to poo-poo the science basis for vaccination. For a doctor who believes in science this is disturbing; for you, a mummy doing the best for your baby, these groups are positively dangerous.

This lobby has very clearly defined motives, and once you understand this, it is easy to see why they don't approve of a public health vaccination programme. Their objectives have nothing to do with the health of your baby and their claims are spurious to say the least. Allow me to explain the most common motives of the anti-vaccine lobby:

- **Motive 1: £££** It won't surprise you to learn that money is a huge motive to form an anti-vaccination group. Some people think 'parent' is a synonym for 'bottomless pit of cash', and people know the quickest way to make you part with that cash is by scaring you. Well, a pretty significant group of the anti-vaccination lobby has cleverly found a way to make money from your fear. This group appears to be concerned about the ingredients in pharmaceutical vaccinations while they are actually peddling 'alternative vaccines'. They claim their au naturel vaccines are harm-free (except to your bank balance). Of course they are harm-free. Harm-free. Science-free. Benefit-free. Except they're not free: someone is making a fortune from selling parents water! They have no value, no proven basis for working and no body of evidence that shows they work. You can find online many groups selling homeopathic vaccines that are incredibly expensive and utterly useless. They are harm-free of course because they are water. These are often given catchy names such as *homeoprophylaxis,* which sounds clever but is actually a synonym for zilch. Anti-vaccination mantras are a clever marketing strategy for this lot.

- **Motive 2: more £££** It won't surprise you to learn another anti-vaccine group is also trying to make money from you. This lot also think your money grows on trees and are equally astute at using your fear as their marketing policy. But this crowd are cunning as their clinics are almost medical and they're using fear to sell you single vaccines rather than the standard-issue ones. These were very popular in the wake of the MMR scandal (see below), and many are still around today flogging their vaccines. Their money is guaranteed if people are unnecessarily afraid of conventional vaccines: a point perfectly illustrated by their prices, which on average include at least a 300 per cent profit.

- **Motive 3: the conspiracists** The internet has given fuel and momentum to the vaccination conspiracy theorists who think vaccination programmes are simply a way for drug companies/governments/doctors to make money. I don't know how this crowd explains the polio phenomenon. Drug companies make money from making drugs: yes, that is a fact, the clue's in the name. Drug companies make huge profits, and we can't ignore that. But the numbers, the lives saved, the eradication of diseases speaks for itself. Pharmaceutical companies may be corporate-behemoths with money as their goal, but if they're saving my kid from death by diphtheria, to be honest I'm okay with that. Drug company profits do not negate the benefits vaccinations produce. Incidentally, I am not, and have never been, paid by a drug company to vaccinate children.

So now you can spot this motley crew of people with your baby's health as their lowest priority. What about all those things they say? Surely, there's something in that. Well, usually not. I have heard and read every single vaccination myth, but I have only chosen to include my top favourites. I just wanted to give you a sense of how ideas can sound scientific even when they are utter hogwash. A bit like using a word like 'homeoprophylaxis'. Sounds good. Means nowt if you understand the science. Here is the *Keep Calm* approach to the most prolific vaccination myths:

1. **Myth: too many vaccinations will overload your baby's immune system**

I can understand why people may think this as many vaccines are given together in our schedule, but it is simply not the case. Your baby's immune system is not one 'catch-all' sieve that can become bottle-necked by a large number of viruses arriving at once to check in. It is a complex array of different cells and different organs in the body that are designed for multiple attacks! More bugs enter a child's immune system when she brushes her teeth or grazes her knee, than from an entire vaccine schedule. It is more challenging for your baby's immune system to sit with you in a coffee shop in winter (and no one sensible would ever suggest you avoid that!), than it is to be vaccinated. Also, vaccinations contain only tiny quantities of virus, and often not the whole virus anyway: it's frequently a casing or 'envelope' just reactive enough to trigger the immune system. Scientific research has proven that your baby's immune system is not overwhelmed by multiple vaccinations.

2. **Myth: vaccines contain mercury, which is a poison**
   This is simply a confusion of the facts surrounding vaccinations. This is a favourite of the money-grabbing crew, desperate to peddle you alternatives. This myth has stemmed from the fact that a compound called thiomersal is used as a preservative in injectable flu vaccines. Thiomersal is a compound that contains a type of mercury called ethylmercury. When ethylmercury gets into our body, it is broken

down very quickly and urinated out, leaving no time for it to be toxic. On the other hand, the scary type of mercury is methylmercury, which is broken down much more slowly and can build up in our bodies: this is the one that can accumulate in fish and can end up being toxic to humans if we eat too much swordfish or tuna, for example. So first of all, it's not a toxic compound to start with because it is ethylmercury not methylmercury. Secondly, not one of the vaccinations on the childhood schedule contains thiomersal anyway – it is mainly found in injectable flu vaccines.

3. **Myth: the MMR vaccination causes autism**
   In the late 1990s a scientific journal published a paper suggesting that MMR could cause autism. Never has a scientific paper been so flawed, gained so much publicity or had such a huge impact on public health. And, unfortunately, such a negative impact. What the paper showed was that the small number of children studied all had autism, and all had received the MMR. What it never proved was any connection or causation. Causation is absolutely vital in medical trials. Many things seem to 'go together', but one may not be *causing* the other. I have curly hair and I love cheese. I have friends who have curly hair and love cheese. That does not prove having curly hair makes you love cheese; it simply shows sometimes you see both characteristics together. The paper was removed, and the author is

no longer allowed to practise as a doctor. No scientific study has ever found a link between autism and MMR: some of the most compelling research comes from Japan where they stopped using MMR but the rates of autism have continued to rise. The truth is that autism symptoms start to appear around the age of 12–18 months, just after babies have routinely had their MMR vaccine. This sad coincidence has allowed the myth to proliferate. We still do not know what causes autism, and it is understandable parents of autistic children look for an answer. That answer is not the MMR vaccine.

4. **Myth: 'My children aren't vaccinated and they've not had any serious illnesses, so it's not really necessary'**
This is a pretty selfish attitude and I can get rather feisty when people say this to me directly. Unvaccinated children in this country are safely living under the blanket of protection I have provided by vaccinating mine. This is called herd immunity. Because our rates of vaccination are thankfully pretty good, there are only low levels of all the scary viruses in the community. It only works when everyone joins in. This is protection en masse and is the only reason unvaccinated children in the UK don't get ill: it is certainly not through any special powers they have. It is crucial to keep up levels of herd immunity to protect those children who for medical reasons (such as cancer) can't be vaccinated. It is also the reason your lovely baby was

protected from scary things when she was still too young to be vaccinated. Unvaccinated children are the first to get ill when there are outbreaks of measles, and are the reason outbreaks of measles occur in the first place. When I meet someone who tries to sell me this myth I always ask them if they fancy taking their unvaccinated children to Nigeria where polio is still endemic? They don't.

Vaccination is a gift parents should accept with open arms. Medical science, global data and history has only ever proven its benefits, not the mythological harms.

- Keep calm, although it will be stressful
- Trust your instinct to do the right thing
- You are the expert when it comes to your baby's health

What all those initials actually stand for

The Primary Immunisations Schedule (the vaccinations children have before they start school) details what vaccination you are taking your baby for and which diseases she will be protected from. A record of these should be kept in her personal health record, also known as her red book.

It is vital all your baby's vaccinations are documented in the red book as well as in her GP notes. This prevents mistakes from happening.

Vaccinations – A Rule Dr Ellie Appreciates!

Age	Vaccine	Illnesses prevented	Worth getting
2 months	• DTaP/IPV/Hib	Diphtheria Tetanus Pertussis (whooping cough) Polio Haemophilus pneumonia and meningitis	Yes
	• Pneumococcal	Pneumococcal meningitis	
	• Rotavirus	Gastroenteritis	
3 months	• DTaP/IPV/Hib	Diphtheria Tetanus Pertussis (whooping cough) Polio Haemophilus pneumonia and meningitis	Yes
	• Men C	Meningitis C	
	• Rotavirus	Gastroenteritis	
4 months	• DTaP/IPV/Hib	Diphtheria Tetanus Pertussis (whooping cough) Polio Haemophilus pneumonia and meningitis	Yes
	• Pneumococcal	Pneumococcal meningitis	
12 months	• Hib/Men C booster	Haemophilus pneumonia and meningitis Meningitis C	Yes
	• MMR	Measles, mumps and rubella	
	• Pneumococcal	Pneumococcal meningitis	

Age	Vaccine	Illnesses prevented	Worth getting
2–3 years	• Flu vaccine	Bronchitis, pneumonia and middle ear infections	Yes
3 years+	• MMR second dose • DTaP/IPV	Pre-school booster	Yes

Although only one of these is called 'meningitis', HiB, MMR, pneumococcus and Men C are all given to protect against meningitis-causing bugs. That is a significant part of the programme dedicated to preventing meningitis. Like I said, it's a gift.

Logistics of vaccinations

That vaccination invitation appears just as you're settled into your mummy role and hopefully feeling a little less crazy. You normally have to have a six- or eight-week check with a GP before your baby can start the schedule, just to ensure she has no medical problems.

I think going for the first set of vaccinations is tough for first-timers and I don't mean the babies. It's genuinely hard for mummies to watch their precious bundle have injections with what looks like a humongous needle going into that scrawny thigh! And, don't forget, it's not just one needle – it's normally two and sometimes three so your nerves of steel are an essential asset at this point.

Of course babies do scream when they are vaccinated, often before the second needle has even gone in, which makes it incredibly distressing all round. I have to admit, on the odd occasion that I vaccinate babies (it's usually done by the nurse in my clinic) even I have to muster up a bit of courage and emotional resilience to cope with it. But the crying and pain is really short-lived especially if you have a boob, bottle or dummy ready for your baby straight after. Many of my patients will schedule vaccinations for just before a feed, so they will be ready for milk as the injections are finished: a great comfort to all babies. And you can treat yourself to cake when you get home. Incidentally, be warned, scheduling the feed with the injection only works if your clinic appointments generally run on time, which is not always the case of course.

Another top tip for the actual appointment is to have a think about the clothes you choose for your baby – I'm less fussed about what you wear. A simple-to-unbutton baby-gro is best; first vaccinations are not the time to be showing off the £100 dress great-Aunt Alice bought her from Harrods. You want an easy-to-take-off outfit that requires minimal human skill or dexterity as you and baby will both be flustered. And at least one of you will be screaming.

It makes sense to take a grandma or daddy or a friend along if you can, for moral support especially the first time. You'll probably still be at that stage when leaving the house is a military operation, so the extra pair of hands certainly won't go unused. Probably worth checking, though, that the chosen helper is actually going to be of use: I vaccinated a two-month-old recently, when mum had accidentally missed her nurse's appointment. I asked her if it was still stressful getting out of the house.

'Not today, to be honest, because I brought my boyfriend with me,' she said.

'Is he parking the car?' I queried, slightly confused that he wasn't in for the big moment.

'Oh no, he's in the waiting room. He can't stand the sight of needles.'

I suppose at least he helped carry the nappy bag. By the time it comes round to the third lot of vaccinations, it's less of a trauma all round: you'll be far calmer and even, dare I say it, pretty blasé about that crying. Just remember vaccinations are a great asset to guilt-free parenting: a short-term pain weighed up against lifelong protection against fatal illnesses.

It is not necessary to treat your baby any differently after she's had a vaccination. She should feed normally, although it is possible you will notice she is a little bit irritable for a day or two afterwards. As a normal side-effect of vaccination, you may notice your baby has a slight temperature, and you can use children's paracetamol suspension to bring this down. At any point if your instinct tells you your baby is not herself or you're worried, speak to the GP straight away. I have noticed many parents now assume (or perhaps they are advised) to give children's paracetamol suspension straight after injections, whether the baby has a temperature or not. This is unnecessary and is certainly not standard medical advice. It is best to wait and see how she is, and be guided by that: most babies are absolutely fine afterwards and require no special measures other than lots of extra cuddles. I stand by the notion it's more stressful for you than her!

Postponing a vaccination is sometimes necessary if your baby has a fever already. You easily catch up on this once your baby is well again, and then just carry on where you left off. Being one or two weeks late doesn't affect the schedule, and while it is not ideal it is pretty common particularly among winter babies and those around older kids who generously pass on their snot. You don't need to postpone a vaccination if your baby has a cough, snot or a cold *without* a temperature.

Finally, always make sure your baby is up to date with the vaccination schedule yourself. It's worth writing the approximate times in the diary for the whole of the first year so you can't miss any: you can't always rely on the clinic to send a reminder so it's best to rely on yourself. The schedule is designed to offer your precious baby the best level of protection, and that can only happen if she completes all the injections.

- Keep calm
- Trust your instinct
- Listen to the baby expert: YOU

Chapter 11

Weaning – From Baby Mush to Three Square Meals

Weaning has become a guideline-writer's paradise. What should be a lovely, messy and overall fun stage of a baby's life has become completely ruined and complicated by a plethora of crazy rules that have served to bamboozle and aggravate mothers as opposed to help them!

I have come to the conclusion that there is a working-party committee on parenting rules, and each year they are set a target of bringing in a new weaning rule. Right now, somewhere tucked away on planet Zogg, they're sitting around a large table developing a rule on which specific variety of potato you should introduce first – a Maris Piper or a King Edward?

So be prepared for lists, rules, advice, paraphernalia, meddlers and confusion galore as you begin your weaning journey with bubba. Arm yourself with sense, instinct and a large tank of humour, so you can actually enjoy being sprayed with parsnip mush and introducing your baby to the joys of food.

In the midst of the crazy, unimportant guidelines there are some pretty important ones – admittedly only a few – but these get lost among all the other rubbish out there. This really highlights why I've got such a bugbear with rules: it's been overdone with weaning to the point of insanity, and so many mums don't know what to believe and what to follow. If you are confused, don't worry, you're in good company: even the rule-makers themselves seem to be confused. I read a proper official leaflet recently that advised 'You must not start solids until six months. If you are starting solids at four months, start with baby rice.' What are you, as a new mum, supposed to make of this baffling drivel? The rules contradict the rules.

Be strong and keep calm. This is no different to any other stage of baby's life when your instinct is all-powerful and will guide you through the swamp. You really have to put on your sensible hat here to stand up to the insane doctrine you will be bombarded with so you are not driven bananas by guidelines. Even supposedly level-headed doctors like me found the whole process perplexing: when my daughter was about seven months old, I rang her dad at work.

'Nowhere sells guava!' I shrieked at him.

'Er, okay. I don't like guava. How come you want guava? You're not pregnant again, are you?'

I wasn't pregnant.

'No, the book says the baby should have guava, that's the next fruit on the weaning list. Today was peaches, tomorrow is guava, but I can't find guavas!'

'Does she need to eat guavas if we don't?' came the timid reply, before he cautiously added, 'Have you ever actually eaten guava?'

Of course he was right but my mummy-brain was so focused on rigid weaning rules I'd ignored my common sense and instinct. My daughter never got the guava, but has managed to end up a perfectly enthusiastic foodie despite this terrible omission.

The whole essence of weaning, or introducing solids, is that your baby goes from a purely milk-fed little thing to a mini-person eating three meals a day, reflecting the food that is generally eaten by your family. This will take around six months probably, but is certainly not a finite process as babies' and toddlers' tastes expand and mature for the next few years. It is not a process designed to make your baby a connoisseur of exotic fruit and all varieties of fresh-water trout. It is a natural progression where his eating and drinking habits develop to mimic yours. It is as much about social and physical development as it is about nutrition and calories.

There is no need for it to be complicated; it is a perfectly natural evolution and it should not be overly regimented. It should be fun. And new. And messy. Yes, get used to mess. If you're precious about your white carpet or white walls, now is the time to get over it, unless you intend feeding your baby every meal in the garden shed (I don't recommend that).

So let's take weaning right back to basics. Let's separate the rules from the opinion and get going with the food. Hopefully, with a large dollop of your very fabulous instinct and a tiny soupçon of advice from me, you can relish the next few months of gourmandise.

- Keep calm: this is fun
- Trust yourself
- You are a fully fledged weaning expert

When to start weaning

Okay, so here we go. And before we've even started, the rules are already confused and conflicting! Yes, before you can even begin, the uncertainty has started about *when* you actually can begin, and really the message is still all over the place.

When I was a baby, solids such as mushy rusks were introduced as early as 12 weeks. When my daughter was born in 2003 solids were introduced at four months. Now we're at six months. Well, I think we're at six months.

The official guidelines rightly suggest solids should be introduced at 'around' six months. The rationale for this is to promote exclusive breastfeeding, and possibly as protection against allergy and infection from solid food. However, in reality many babies are weaned earlier than this and this earlier weaning is endorsed by healthcare professionals, such as health visitors and GPs. Confused? Yes, you should be. Here we have an official guideline from the Department of Health, yet currently we think around three-quarters of babies are weaned earlier than that and we say that is okay. So what is going on?

I'll try to explain the contradiction. I think because the guidelines have changed so much, many of us are still used to babies weaning earlier, and have generally seen no problems from babies weaned a few weeks before their half birthday. So while we wouldn't tell you to start early, if you come to us and you've already started, we're not going to call social services because we know you've probably not caused any harm. There has not been any science to show it is harmful if solids are started before six months if parents think their babies are ready. Also, the guideline to wait until six months is not to prevent something deadly serious (compared to, say, the rule about putting your baby on his back to sleep to prevent cot death, for example), it is more to promote exclusive breastfeeding and avoid allergies. So if mums feel their baby is ready and want to start earlier we go against the rule and say, go ahead.

Babies are individuals and just as in every other arena you cannot define exactly when they will be ready. The guidelines, in fairness, does state 'around' six months and as we know all babies are different. I am still seeing the majority of my patients start weaning their babies on to solids at 5½–6 months and it seems to work absolutely fine. You will know when your baby is ready – he will be staring longingly at your lasagne and putting all manner of things into his mouth – you'll see he's just waiting for that glorious food. If you think your baby is ready and it's about the right time, go for it!

If there is to be a definitive rule, it is not to start before 17 weeks, which really is far too early. Your baby has to be sitting up okay to be able to eat solid food – it's hard to feed solids to a baby slouched on a baby bouncer and, likewise, he has to have developed the swallowing and co-ordination to take solids. When you start too early, you see that babies push the food out and gag.

In babies with proven allergies, eczema, or a strong family history of allergy we would definitely want you to chat through weaning your baby with your doctor or health visitor as some rules about *what* and *when* do come into play.

The practicalities

I could tell you to buy certain spoons, certain bowls and a highchair that does cartwheels in 84 different positions, and why plastic bibs are superior to paper ones. But I won't, because the truth is absolutely none of it matters at all. There is a variety of feeding paraphernalia, but what you buy and whether it ends up being useful is a matter for you. Babies have to enjoy eating, and part of that is being interested in the meals. If that means musical Thomas the Tank Engine plates, then so be it. YOU also have to find feeding and weaning fun, so buy whatever makes life easy for you: there's no point getting an overly complicated highchair with so many crevices that it is arduous to clean, because it will turn weaning into a hassle. And this is supposed to be fun, not hard labour!

My daughter was given a lovely Beatrix Potter baby cutlery set when she was born, which was very beautiful. It is still very beautiful a decade later because it has never been used: largely due to the fact it has the words 'Not suitable for the dishwasher' printed on the box. Get simple, non-expensive, easy-to-clean things that are practical. You don't want to be spending time scraping avocado mush from intricate porcelain.

Possibly the most useful thing you can buy yourself is a giant tub of washing powder and a mop because you will certainly need it. Weaning is messy, and you will be amazed at where you find food mush stuck. Just for added fun, it gets a lot messier when you start to let your baby feed himself. This is an important little developmental stage that will happen at some point, and you'll have to learn to be Zen about mess.

Talking of cleaning, what about sterilising? Up until now anything that goes into your baby's mouth should have been sterilised. Milk bottles and expressing machine parts are particularly important as they have tiny nooks that are impossible to clean and leftover stinky milk is a great breeding ground for bugs. Even once your baby is sticking carpet fluff and dog toys in his mouth, it still makes sense to sterilise the milk bottles because of that. It's not such a hassle and there should be fewer bottles as he gets older. As far as sterilising the other weaning bits goes, it's entirely up to you. The cutlery, bowls and plates you use need to be scrupulously clean, but beyond that be guided by your baby; if he's sticking all manner of dirty objects from the floor into his mouth, it's not really going to be worth sterilising a spoon.

- Trust yourself to wean him
- Learn from your baby
- You can't really go wrong

The honest action plan for weaning

Keep calm, it's very simple! If you understand the principles of weaning as a taste-and-texture evolution you are unlikely to need lists and didactic regulations of exact foods to give. This is about a concept of changing your baby's feeding habits over a period of time. Here's the deal: your little one is going to go from tiny tastes of soft, puréed, simple food to eating good-sized, mini-meals that involve all food groups. It's a process. Most babies will take about six months, some will take more, some less. How fast or slow you take it is entirely dependent on how your baby takes to solids, and what he's ready for.

The progression is as much about introducing textures as it is about introducing flavours and different food groups, i.e. proteins, carbohydrates and fats. So over the six or so months it takes, your baby will evolve through textures, tastes and portion sizes until he's eventually feeding himself three meals a day that vaguely resemble something a human would eat for breakfast, lunch and dinner.

If you like tables (I secretly do), it would look like this for weaning principles:

	At the start	At the end
Texture	Liquidy, runny purée	Normal-looking, lumpy food
Food type	Basic bland tastes	All food groups
Quantity	1–2 teaspoons a day	3 square meals a day
Who does the feeding	You	Him

You start with the simplest foods and work your way up. Likewise you start with the mushiest and gradually get lumpier. The easiest way to think about the progress is in a plan of three parts each lasting around a couple of months-ish:

Step 1

This is bland mush (don't tell him that). You're starting with baby rice, fruit and vegetables and at this stage the texture of everything is very runny. Most fruit and veg will need cooking to make it soft enough to purée, although not banana or avocado of course. Start with baby rice mixed with some of your baby's usual milk, then add in fruit and veggies: potatoes (any variety), pears, apples, bananas, carrots, peaches, peas, broccoli, really any root or green veggies will work. You can even give him guava if you want. The food should be very puréed, very mushy and very colourful. To him this will be a whole new world of fun tastes. Some he'll like and some he won't. Once he's getting into it you can mix together some combinations. This is about tasting, and feeling, and trying the new flavours. He might not like peas one week, but like them the next. Don't give up after a first attempt: it's always worth having a second go as his tastebuds evolve.

It makes sense to try one food – for example, just carrot purée – for a few days to make sure your baby is okay with it, before trying something new. Let's say you started carrot and apple on the same day and he had a reaction (unlikely), you wouldn't know which food was the culprit.

It will take you a few weeks to have a go at trying lots of different foods. You don't need to sample every vegetable in the local farmers' market – just a reasonable variety to make it interesting for your baby.

If you have started weaning before six months, it is advisable not to start step 2 until he has turned six months. This is because when we start step 2, you are introducing more of the 'allergenic' food groups, such as wheat and eggs and cow's milk, and his body needs to be that bit more mature to handle them.

Step 2

At step 2, you take things up a notch in terms of flavours and textures. Learning to cope with textures is a big part of weaning: once you're a couple of months in, the purées can be less runny and more mashed with some little soft bits. Babies learn to deal with lumps once they're comfortable chewing, so it's important to graduate from purées, through little soft bits, to fully fledged lumps. If you scale up in this way, you are not putting him at risk of choking: I know many mums are afraid of this. Follow your baby's lead. Remember it's a process: you're scaling up from purées to something that resembles adult food gradually over a few months. This is a developmental process: babies are not born knowing how to chew. Once he's confident and you are happy he can chew soft lumps, you might even want to try soft finger foods such as little pieces of banana he can try and pop in himself (don't worry, his aim won't be great to start with).

The food now gets more interesting. You can start adding in protein in the form of meat, fish, lentils or beans, which can be puréed with veg to start with. Well-cooked eggs, and cheese and full-fat dairy yoghurts, as well as soft mushy pasta and soft squidgy toast, are all great options. Well-cooked soft scrambled egg is the perfect consistency for the soft little bits in a meal. You can add in mushy versions of the carbohydrates you have at home including bread and cereals, as well as posh things like cous cous, which quite frankly is perfect baby food. Baby porridge is a good staple as are other mainstream cereals like Weetabix. His meals will now have little portions of carbohydrates, proteins and fats, as well as the lovely fruit and vegetables.

Your baby's diet by the end of this stage will be quite varied with protein hopefully on most days, as well as a range of carbs, fruit and green things. You can take this as slow or as fast as you like: there are lots of things to try out there, and there's no hurry. As long as you're working with your baby to try new tastes and new textures, you can't go wrong.

Step 3

Another two months-ish down the line and you can explore a much wider variety of finger food. Texture-wise your baby will be learning to go with lumps, and food will gradually start to look how it does when *you* eat it. Finger food can be anything that your baby is able to chew: try soft buttered toast, pieces of banana, small pieces of cooked vegetables, grated cheese and pieces of cooked pasta. Rice cakes, pieces of cereal, little soft pieces of chicken are all perfect because they are fun for your baby to learn to pick up, and they go soft very easily in his mouth. Once your baby gets used to these foods, you can introduce firmer foods such as pieces of cucumber, mini-sandwiches, breadsticks or dried fruit that he can chew little bits off. His meals will contain all the food groups, but will be a combination of foods he can handle himself, such as peas to pick up and toast to suck, as well as lumpy foods such as porridge or pasta and sauce that you feed him.

And that is it: so around six or so months after you've started, you'll have your own little gastronome eating a variety of different food types in all shapes and sizes with a large proportion of it still ending up in his hair (and yours).

- Keep calm
- Trust yourself to feed him properly
- Enjoy the mess

Timing and portion sizes

When you start weaning, it is all about tasting tiny quantities, and milk is still the mainstay of your baby's diet. At the end of your journey he'll be on three meals a day with at most 2–3 milk feeds. So how do you get from one to the other?

Well, it's an easy journey and you can really do this however you like. When you start weaning, it makes sense to start in the morning or at lunchtime-ish: you're fresh, he's fresher and then you've got the rest of the day to see if he has any reaction to the food you gave. Just give little tastes, 1–2 teaspoons at the most, either before or during a milk feed. This isn't about calories at this stage, so the milk still takes priority. Once he's used to those foods, say after a week or two, you can start to create a second little solids session too, and then gradually a third until he's essentially having some solids at the times he'd be having meals when he's a big boy. It doesn't matter if he has veg for breakfast and cereal for dinner; structure it however you like into a model that you can see will resemble your family's eating patterns.

As far as portion sizes go, you start with a teaspoon and at the end of your weaning journey he's having a baby meal. What size is a baby meal? It depends on the size of your baby! The problem with setting out specific amounts is that all babies are different, and each day is different. If you gradually work up from a teaspoon or so you will be fine. Watch to see how much he wants and never ever force him to take more. If he is spitting or pushing it out, that's a very clear message that needs little explanation.

The first few weeks he'll take only a spoon or two at any given time, especially as he needs tummy room for his milk. Gradually he'll take more, until he's having a bowlful – although that depends on the size of your bowls. It's all about guess-timating. Follow him and his cues, and your own instinct. This is about learning together and trusting yourselves. There is not one baby-portion that is right for all babies so you'll have to be guided by your own unique foodie to see how much he wants. You can't go wrong.

Fussy eaters

I see a lot of parents who worry their baby seems to be a fussy eater or a bit particular about which fruits they like and which meat they will try. In an effort to give your baby numerous options and open up to him the world of gastronomy, you shouldn't forget that actually he might not like everything that is put in front of him. If you compared your baby to many adults, you'd see they are actually pretty similar: most of us eat the same few fruits and vegetables all the time and only branch out every so often. We're all a bit fussy about our food and babies have a right to be the same! Of course you can offer your baby many types of food but if he only likes a few I really don't think that is a cause for concern. It's not uncommon for a mum to come in and say to me their baby is very fussy but when we go through all the foods they DO eat, it's actually a good enough range. If you are worried you have a fussy foodie, try out this little action plan for dealing with it:

1. Make a list of all the foods he does eat, rather than concentrate on the ones he doesn't. Most parents are reassured when they see this list as long as it contains a few from each food group.

2. Don't give up. Babies are terribly fickle with food and may hate avocados one day and love them a

few months later. Remember this is a developmental process and tastebuds can mature and change.

3. Try foods in different ways. He may not like potatoes mashed but he might like them boiled: it may seem the same to us, but it could be the texture rather than the taste he disapproves of.

4. Chill out. While weaning starts now, it's by no means a finite process. A baby can be discerning in his tastes to start with but still go on to try and enjoy new foods as he grows up. Being 'fussy' at 10 months certainly doesn't mean he'll be fussy at 10 years.

What about all that lovely milk?

Over the course of his weaning voyage, his milk intake will definitely reduce but it certainly doesn't stop. In the beginning when you're just tasting and trying, the milk feeds won't be affected at all. Gradually as the puréed meals scale up in size over a month or two, the milk feeds will start to reduce.

Along the whole process, you'll find your baby probably drops 2–3 feeds. Like I always say, this really depends on your own little one. Some babies get so hooked on interesting solids, the bland white stuff just doesn't cut it any more, and they're dropping down pretty quickly. Others love their milk so they don't want to give up on it so easily, and you may even have to intentionally give him less milk so there's room in his tummy for mush.

Up until a year, milk (whether breast or fomula) is still

incredibly important for nutrition and calories so make sure your baby is still having at least 2–3 milk feeds a day. He can start drinking normal full-fat cow's milk at a year, but until then his baby milk is far more suited to his needs.

Weaning certainly does not mean you should be weaning off breastfeeding, and many breastfeeding mothers continue quite happily alongside solid foods. This is perfectly normal. Six months of breastfeeding is fantastic, and it's entirely up to you whether you carry on regardless or take solids as your cue to stop. Just like with bottle-feeds, the volume your baby has starts to go down so you will notice your supply adjusts accordingly. Because the changes are so gradual, and you're not suddenly dropping any feeds dramatically, you shouldn't notice any pain or discomfort. Breasts are particularly clever: once they feel there is less demand at certain times, they know to make less milk. Gosh, us girls are perfectly designed aren't we?

As you start your weaning journey, your baby is also going to learn there are other drinks besides milk and you get to experiment with the joy that is the *sippy cup*. Never in your life will you be faced with so many options: cups that don't spill, magical valves, self-cleaning, self-opening, self-emptying: you name it, you can get it in a sippy cup. Just remind yourself this is essentially a cup with a lid. The sheer number of different contraptions to give your kid water are astounding, but the reality is if he is going to get used to drinking water, he needs it to be easy. And you need to be able to clean the damn thing. I notice the mums I look after all end up with the simplest cups because that means baby actually gets some water. Yes, some of it spills while he's learning, but given the mess you're now accustomed to, spilt water is no big deal.

Water is the safest, cheapest, easiest drink to offer your baby. It doesn't have any sugar and giving him a bland drink means it won't change the taste of the solid food he's getting used to: having a sweet drink can make veggies taste more bitter, which doesn't help him get used to food.

So water is the best thing to give him? Yes, but only if he actually takes it. There is no point offering him water exclusively which he refuses, so he ends up with hard, dehydrated poos from not drinking enough. If he consistently refuses water from all manner of super-duper cups, it is perhaps worth adding in a splash of apple juice so at least he drinks some fluids with his mini-meals. Giving diluted apple juice is not going to harm him and the quantity of sugar he will get if you dilute it is, quite frankly, tiny. Of course it's best if he takes water, but there's no point being militant about it if he ends up drinking nothing. You don't need to feel guilty because you didn't produce a water-drinker as lots of babies don't like water, and he's got plenty of time to try it when he's older.

So which weaning rules are worth following?

While I don't really believe in food lists for weaning, there are certainly a few essential rules to follow. I even think these boil down to common sense, but they are worth spelling out.

- No salt thank you, babies don't need it and their kidneys won't like it.
- No sugar or sweetener needs to be added to anything.
- Honey should not be given before a year as it can cause botulism (nasty).
- Babies don't need low-fat food. Full-fat cheese/yoghurt, etc., are best.

And that's it.

Remember it's not all about the food

Weaning is not just about eating and drinking. It is an important part of development that has as much to do with social development as it does learning to chew.

At some point, it makes sense that your little one will want or need to feed himself, and learning this all begins from the start of weaning. It is massively unlikely that your six-month-old is going to be able to aim any food into the correct orifice straight away, but you certainly have to give him the chance to try. Yes, most of it will end up on the floor, and yes, a lot will get wasted but in the meantime he's learning self-sufficiency and important co-ordination. This is why I said be Zen about mess. Of course, if you feed him all the time there'll be less mess and no wastage, but he's not learning to look after himself.

Once you're on your happy weaning journey, give him a spoon too. Let him have a go. Let him stick his finger in the mush and taste it for himself. Babies learn this stuff by mimicry, and it's natural for him to want to put things into his mouth himself. Of course he won't get the fromage frais in the right place entirely without your help, so work as a team. It might seem weird for you to think about it now, but soon he's going to be running into the kitchen getting the food for himself, so you've got to teach him the right skills. If you let him start, when weaning starts, by giving him his own spoon (which, yes, most of the time will end up in his eye), he'll easily learn how to feed himself. You're a long way off from him making his own lunch, but it really is a first step.

What about allergies?

Food allergies are certainly far more common than they once were, or perhaps we're just more aware of them and clued up. But that doesn't mean you need to be scared of them. Most babies are allergic to nothing and safely wean on to all foods. In a child with no risks of allergy, there is no reason to suspect he will have one. So you don't have to be concerned about your baby being allergic to foods unless there is already cause for concern in the allergy arena such as:

- He's already been diagnosed with a food allergy.
- He's already got eczema.
- You're an allergic family with a history of eczema or food allergies.

In these cases you should certainly speak to your GP about what you should avoid and be cautious of. Otherwise, the allergenic foods such as eggs, milk, soy, wheat and fish can all be safely introduced between 6–12 months. Science has proven that delaying giving these foods isn't necessary. It is worth taking it slowly with these types of food, and introducing them in mini-amounts initially, but most children will be absolutely fine. Trying small quantities early in the day, over a few days, allows you to experiment, with little risk from a massive allergic reaction. The same even goes for peanut and sesame products, as well as berries and citrus fruit: restricting them completely is not necessary – you just need to sample them in small quantities to make sure your baby doesn't have an allergic reaction. (Whole nuts should never be given until your child is five because they are a choking hazard.)

Coping with the 'masterchef' mummies

Have you got used to competitive mummies yet? I hope so. Just in case they're still making you feel inadequate, here's a dash of advice to help you keep calm. Competitive mums love weaning. It's a wondrous arena for the show-offs around:

- 'Harry eats all type of bream and his favourite grain is quinoa.'
- 'It's wonderful Jamie has never eaten a single pouch, I just love making fresh food every day.'

I once even met a mum who made her own baby rice. Don't ask. You will hear fantastical tales of babies who eat the most exotic fruit and absolutely adore all varieties of squash (the vegetable I mean, not Ribena). I wouldn't take notice of any of it. Firstly, a great deal of these pronouncements are rather – well, let's be diplomatic – exaggerated. And secondly, it doesn't matter what the baby next door eats for breakfast if yours is perfectly happy and content eating his.

You follow your own weaning agenda for your family. Of course it's nice if your little one enjoys the food you spend hours blending, but he's not going to love all of it and that's fine. You're always going to be faced with people whose babies appear to be superior beings, or mummies who claim they've done weaning better than anyone else.

Weaning is not a competitive sport, and is certainly not something to feel guilty about, as you can't really do it wrong. Of course there's going to be days when you give him a jar or pouch of ready-made mush. Quite frankly, I don't actually believe those mothers who say they don't. Do what is right for your family and your baby, and as always ignore the interferers and the meddlers. Trust yourself on this, just like everything else.

- Keep calm
- Trust your instinct
- Listen to the baby expert: YOU

Chapter 12
What Now? – Starting the Next Stage of Your Life

A fter the craziness of the first few months with your baby, and your metamorphosis into super-mamma extraordinaire, there will come a time when you may think, what now? I don't mean, 'What now? Do we have to go to baby gym *again*?' I mean the gargantuan, 'WHAT NOW? Where is my life going?' Some mothers will ask themselves this after a mere few months in their new mummy-role: I know one mother who was thinking this even before the placenta was delivered. For others it may take a few years until you even contemplate life outside the world of muslins, mush and mess.

I realised I was ready to go back to work when one day on maternity leave I asked my husband what type of bread he thought I should bake while he was at work. I don't know which one of us was more surprised. Once I'd teleported myself back from the 1950s, I looked for a job.

The reality for most mummies is that the very simple question 'What now?' will most likely have a very complex answer. There are no rules about working, despite what plenty of people will tell you, but it is probably the hugest guilt-inducing part of this motherhood-lark. Wherever you end up you have to be so strong to protect yourself from feeling like a failure at one (or all) aspects of your life. With a bit of sense, and plenty of your wonderful instinct, you'll be fully armed and fully prepared to enter this next exciting juncture. If you've made it through the mayhem and lunacy of the early days of motherhood, I'm sure you've built up the vigour to navigate the madness of the 'What now?' decision.

- Keep calm, this is certainly not easy
- Listen to yourself
- Trust yourself to make the right decision for your family

It's not really much of a choice is it?

To put it bluntly, not really, no. There's no point being rosy-eyed about this.

We live in a very different world to that of our grannies who stayed at home while their kids played at their feet. Nowadays us girls are supposed to have a 'choice' – we can work, we're educated, we can do what we want. So that makes our lives easier, right? Oh no, sister! While those suffragettes did us a massive favour, modern mothers are stuck in a big balancing act juggling several balls in the air at once. So prepare yourself to make the biggest no-choice choice of your life.

Very few mums are in the enviable position of being able to make this enormous decision based on nothing other than their own personal choice. Whatever is portrayed in magazines and newspapers, making this decision is quite plainly not black and white: there is far more to it than simply doing what your heart wants to do. Life is far, far too complicated in the 21st century for this to be a straightforward decision, and so many factors come into the equation.

If it were simply a case of your inclination, life would be downright straightforward. But 10,000 other issues come into play, not least childcare costs, your career path, your workplace, family support, childcare availability, your feelings, the mortgage, the rent, your salary, your partner's salary, the cost of living, your job spec., grand-parent availability, etc. Even society's expectations of motherhood will have an effect on this so-called *choice*.

From looking after many a mummy, I have seen that the vast number of women have very little choice in when and how they go back to work. Many of my patients can't afford to go back to work due to the strangling costs of childcare and have to leave the working world for a few years. Likewise other patients can't afford *not* to work because of the rising cost of living, even though they want to be at home with their babies. Single mums rarely have the luxury of making these choices; and those with far-flung families who aren't readily available to help also find it all gets very tricky. What appears to be a choice actually ends up as very little choice.

And while I'm on my soap-box having a mini-rant for a

moment, let me tell you another reason why it isn't easy for us super-mummies: parents living in the UK do not have it easy as far as work/home balance is concerned. Although we are now moving towards a more flexible 'shared parental leave' system rather than simply maternity leave, longer-term flexible career paths for women (and men) are still a rarity. Those families who find organising their work/home balance easy are really the very lucky exceptions. Childcare provision is getting better, *but* it is still vastly under-appreciated and successive governments have really not made it easy for families. You only need to look at countries like Sweden where childcare is consistently good and cheap, and fathers routinely share parental leave with mothers, to see we are a long way as a society from getting it right. So if you're feeling you're caught between a rock and a hard place navigating this big not-much-of-a-choice choice, blame the government. They are the ones that should be feeling guilty about all this, not us mummies!

You have to trust yourself to make it work for your family and your baby. You'll have to be honest about what is feasible as well as what you want to do.

Prepare for the dreaded opinions

Leaving your baby to go to work or leaving your career to bring up your baby would make any rational woman feel guilty, thinking about what they 'should' be doing. I hear this so often from mummies, no matter where their life has ended up:

- 'I'll feel terrible if I go back to work. How can I leave my baby all day?'
- 'I'll feel terrible abandoning my career. What was the point of all that training?'

We're geared up for guilt: it's one of the million things we're brilliant at.

But then on top of this natural guilt us mummies are blessed with, some clever commentators/experts/meddlers have developed the whole notion of the 'working-mothers' debate, in an effort to make the mummy-guilt just that bit worse. Thanks very much guys! Yes, despite the fact most of us have very little choice in what happens next, there is one enormous 'working-mothers' debate boiling away and ready to pounce on you just when you feel at peace with the situation you're in.

Avoid articles that are headlined, 'Why working mothers are to blame…' or 'stay-at-home mothers are to blame…'. In my mind these are the most damaging, fundamentally brainless articles based on a woman's choice for her own family. Considering how far the feminist movement and women have come in the last 100 years, I find it quite astounding that editors still publish such articles. In the decade since I became a mother, I have caught sight of nearly 300 articles on this subject, none of which make any sense whatsoever. From the moment you start reading, you are made to feel instantly guilty about what is essentially a decision involving your family and your family ONLY.

If you believed everything you read about working

mothers, apparently we're responsible for damn near every crisis that has struck Earth from the Great Fire of London to the latest earthquake in Japan. Single-handedly, working mammas cause asthma, allergy, behavioural issues in cats and the rise in divorce rates in the UK. It wouldn't surprise me to open the papers one day and read that working mothers are responsible for the destruction of the polar ice caps – after all, if they didn't use all that carbon getting to work ...

Well, it is all a load of absolute rubbish and these articles are damaging, degrading and unnecessarily guilt-inducing. The pseudo-research that is often cited is absolute hogwash at best and should really not even be given the title 'research'. I'd be embarrassed to use these articles as chip-paper. (If I ate chips, of course.)

Given that women can't as yet split themselves in two, and trial one half at home with baby and the other half going to work, how can any science prove anything about working mothers? You cannot design a controlled experiment to observe what would happen to your family over 10 years if you went to work, while at the same time looking at your family if you didn't. What you read about are merely generalisations of what pseudo-experts *think* about working mothers.

Scientific research has never proven anything at all about the pros and cons of staying at home as a mother or going to work, and you mustn't be sucked into the codswallop that is pretending to be science.

- Listen to the expert on your family: YOU
- If it works for your family, it is right
- Ignore the guilt-mongers

Public opinion on working mothers and stay-at-home mothers is based on biased attitudes, personal experience and often the male ideal of what a mother should be. Now, I'm certainly no bra-burning feminist (always seemed to me like a waste of good underwear), but there is no one who knows what is right for you and your family, except you and your family.

I might have to create a rule here for the sake of your sanity, and your brilliance: never ever read commentaries on working mothers versus stay-at-home mothers.

Generalising about the benefits of working or the disadvantages of staying at home, does nothing for women, super-mums or society as a whole. They just serve to cause guilt and sadness: there is no 'debate' about what mothers should be doing. Right now commit yourself to making sure you ignore all the interferers and meddlers who seek to impose their views on you. They're the very same people who comment on the way you feed or soothe your baby, so I hope you've stopped listening to them by now.

This is important, for you to feel comfortable with your life and your family. This decision is tough enough, without taking into account the feelings of those who are completely irrelevant. No one can or should dictate whether or not it is right for you to stay at home or become a working mother.

Listen to yourself and those people who care about

you, to help you navigate what you will do next. It is certainly not easy with massive financial and logistical decisions to make, but you have the instinct to make the right moves; don't let it be drowned out. Trust yourself and while it may not be easy to work out what to do next, at least you can be comfortable with your own path. Your baby doesn't need a working mother or a stay-at-home mother. She just needs a mother. Full stop.

There is fundamentally no difference between those mums that work and those that don't. All mothers should be empowered in their life-path and supported in the decision you take for YOUR family.

You know what? Some people are just not cut out to stay at home all day, sculpt Play-Doh and build Lego towers. It is only human, however, much as we love our babies, to want time to yourself. Whether it be 10 minutes to shower by yourself or a whole day at work.

There are a thousand different types of good mother and choosing to go back to work does not mean you lose that accolade. Many working mothers feel better for working: they feel it gives them self-esteem and creates a role model they want for their kids. Satisfaction from work is very different to satisfaction from home, and craving that is not something to feel guilty about. This does not mean you have failed as a mother: it simply means you're listening to yourself and doing what is right.

To say you enjoy working is not to say you don't enjoy motherhood. The two are not mutually exclusive. It is a balance and, while society might dictate otherwise, not all parents want to be with their children all the time. This is not something a man would ever be questioned about or made to feel inferior about.

Of course children need their mothers, I'm not saying they don't. What I'm saying is that by working you are not giving up being a mother. You're just choosing to juggle both. This is not failure. Going back to work does not negate your achievements as super-mother extraordinaire. In fact it makes it hugely impressive if you can juggle both.

- Listen to yourself and what you want
- Try it, it's not forever
- Trust your instinct

At the other end of the spectrum, if you choose to be – or just end up being – a stay-at-home mamma that is a fabulous and significant role. Stay-at-home mothers are completely and utterly undervalued and it is very offensive and aggravating. You are not bowing out of feminism if you stay at home to nurture your family. You have no apologies to make if you are devoting your days to your family, rather than a career: I get very upset when I hear about women made to feel guilty for 'abandoning' their careers to stay at home. Being a stay-at-home mum is certainly not an easy option, and quite frankly I admire mummies with the dedication and strength this job takes. And yes it is a job, the same as any other, except it's much harder because it's 24 hours a day.

Defining yourself as a stay-at-home mum can be really tough due to the assumptions people make about you and the misconception that it's easy or you're somehow lazy.

Staying at home does not mean you have failed at a career. You have not dumped feminism if you choose to stay home to bring up your baby. Feminism was supposed to be about giving women choices, not dictating which choices you must make.

There isn't much glory in being a stay-at-home mum, which makes it even harder to get used to. Just like working mums you end up being judged for your choice, whether you've had any choice in the matter or not.

You are the expert on your family and you have to trust yourself to make things work. Listen to your instinct and, despite all the opinions, keep calm.

This decision is not for life

Things will change enormously for you over the next few years. The days when you were stuck at home covered in vomit and breast milk will seem a distant memory when you're in the park chasing a toddler who has just pooped in her big-girl knickers for the 19th time.

Life over the next few years is a constant roller coaster in terms of you and your baby and your little family. And, blimey, you'll probably even contemplate more children, and go through the whole barmy process all over again.

The decisions you make early on about working or staying at home are not for life. At most they are for a year or two; this is certainly not set in stone. You are not signing up to a lifelong membership of the stay-at-home gang or working-mums club.

It's trial and error really: it is so normal for mummies to change paths and not end up where they were intending. What may seem like an impossible work–home balance in the beginning might just get easier and you may relish your time in the office. The logistics might prove easier than you thought, or much, much harder. The take-home pay might end up pointless for the effort you're putting in, and you'll give up. You may work a couple of days, realise you love it, and step up to working more. You may have thought you wanted to carry on with the rat race, but actually real-ise you'd rather be at home finger-painting.

Consider this next step to be merely a trial. This will really help you to keep calm about the whole thing. You're just going to try it and see how it feels. You really have no idea how you will feel and how circumstances may change. Yet again in your journey through motherhood, you have to get used to being flexible. This is a time to listen to yourself and that instinct so you can keep calm and follow the right path for you.

Of course you will agonise about these decisions: quite frankly you'd be pretty weird if you didn't. Leaving your baby. Giving up your career. Choosing childcare. These are not minor decisions to make, but don't drive yourself too mad. Things change and you are not planning the next 10 years, probably the next two years if you're lucky.

I look after mummies right through their pregnancy and many have a very fixed idea of what they will do about work in their new role. But I see pregnant women who live for work who then completely change path and stay at home for years with their kids. Who we are before parenthood can be very different to who we are after. This is no bad thing. It is evolution and a metamorphosis to celebrate.

The next few years for your little family will be exciting, busy and fun. Go with the flow, you don't know how things will change and how you will all feel: the most high-powered businesswoman I ever knew, who was texting the office while waiting for her cervix to dilate, was so enthralled by motherhood she extended her maternity leave by a whole year, and then never went back. She's ended up deliriously content with her five (yes, I did say five) kids and her dog. And she's the first to admit, no one is more surprised by what happened to her than she is!

In the 10 years that I have been a mother, I've tried it all: I've had periods of working full-time, working part-time and not working at all. The decisions I have taken have had very little to do with personal choice, but a great deal to do with cash flow, my career ladder and the available childcare. Sometimes the balance has felt perfect (well, two days in a decade to be honest), sometimes it felt completely wrong, but more often than not it feels kind-of okay.

You will find what works for your family and your circumstances. And sometimes it won't work, and you will move on and try something else. That is life and the reality of parenthood. Enjoy.

Which childcare is right?

Once again, you're going to have to make a decision that is not simply a case of choice but will depend on cash, availability and flexibility. But beyond that are there rules on which childcare is best? Of course not. Is it better to choose nursery or a childminder or a nanny or a granny? Well, as you might suspect there are genuinely no rules because it all comes down to personal choice and family logistics. What will be the perfect childcare for me and my baby will be completely wrong for you and yours. There is no right or wrong as far as childcare is concerned. Although many people try to argue otherwise, you can't dictate whether nurseries are better than nannies, or nannies are better than a childminder.

Sure, people will harp on about nurseries being best because the babies socialise, or childminders being optimal because they mix different-age children, but this all boils down to opinion. Of course babies socialise more in a nursery and there's a lot of structure and scheduled activities. That makes them a great choice for many families: for others, they'd rather the smaller, homelier environment of a childminder or the comfort of being at home with a nanny with one-on-one attention. One is not better than another in general terms, only in terms of what is better for your baby. Trust yourself to make that decision for your family.

All childcare has downsides and savvy mums need to be realistic about that too. Nurseries can be pretty inconvenient through the winter as they can have very strict 'snot' policies, and may reject your baby on days when she's snotty even if she's otherwise perfectly well. That's fine if you have an understanding boss, but can get rather awkward if you don't. I've always thought grannies are the perfect nannies and with my first baby was lucky enough to use that option. But I've had more than one mummy moan to me about Granny-nanny who doesn't listen to instructions and feeds the baby too much chocolate. (Mine was clearly better trained.) All childcare has downsides and upsides; you have to weigh those up for yourself as you are the expert on your baby.

For most families the choice of childcare is limited by logistics, particularly cost and convenience: getting yourself to work and baby settled for the day is stressful enough so convenience is a massive part of the equation. There is no point choosing what others cite as the 'best nursery in town', if said nursery adds extra miles to your morning rush hour and puts you into overdraft. That makes it the worst nursery in town for you.

If you are in the position to have a degree of choice, you choose what is right for your family and your baby. You have to listen to yourself and be guided by your instinct. It goes without saying you have to leave your baby somewhere you know she will be safe, comfortable and happy. And you have to be confident and secure in that choice, so you can keep calm about leaving her.

That first day without you: it's hard

Whatever you decide to do as far as childcare is concerned, you will have to face that *first* day without your baby. She will be absolutely fine, and you will be a complete wreck.

I hate to break it to you but while you're crying into your latte at the thought of leaving her, she will be more than content in her new environment, with other babies to lick and mountains of exhilarating toys to break. You on the other hand will feel bereft and heartbroken, guilt-ridden at leaving her to have so much fun while you slog your guts out. Children are fickle little things and the allure of new all-singing toys and paints to cover themselves in, will overshadow that separation anxiety very quickly. And while that may be hard for your ego to take, it's all perfectly normal.

Whether you're leaving your baby with Granny or a childminder, you'll have to get used to walking away and letting someone else be in control. She may have a few wobbles at the beginning, but it doesn't take long for most little ones to feel settled. And, believe me, while you're standing at the photocopier pining for her, she's having a whale of a time.

Different places have different settling-in policies (that probably doesn't apply to grandparents), but it makes massive amounts of sense to start settling your baby a good few weeks before you need to. You'll feel less stressed about it if you've got plenty of time to settle her in and some babies can take time to get used to a new routine, however much they enjoy it. I would even have settling-in days if you are lucky enough to have family as childcare: you all still need to get used to the childcare situation and having a couple of practice runs is not a bad plan. Even if it's really just a practice run for YOU to get used to leaving your baby and that weird feeling of someone else being responsible for her, it's a good idea.

Letting up on yourself

When you're juggling working and motherhood, you've got to go a bit easy on yourself. Just like in the first few crazy weeks of parenthood, which will now seem like a distant memory, you have to be realistic about what you can achieve within the 24 hours a day that you've got. You can still be a super-mamma and a super-woman, but give yourself a break. You don't have to be a perfectionist. It is exhausting mentally and physically especially in the beginning of a new phase and you have to give everything time to settle.

No matter how much you try, there will be times when you don't feel like you're doing work or home properly and that is fine. This is so normal and you mustn't be hard on yourself. Ask yourself, if you're working and trying to spend as much time as possible with your little one, is it essential to be baking that birthday cake from scratch? Well, if you enjoy it and it's relaxing for you to be covered in flour and icing then, yes, it probably is a good use of your very limited free time. But if it becomes a massive stress and you're turning the oven on at 1 am, then give up and send your other half down to Sainsbury's.

Likewise I have mums who say to me they are finding it hard to get to the gym in between nursery drop-offs and work. They're upset with themselves for not having the energy and feeling guilty about not exercising. Give yourself a break! There is only so much one person can do and you need the energy to concentrate on the important things: your family and yourself.

Just as you did in those first few weeks of motherhood, go easy on those expectations you have of yourself. This is not the time to be proving your worth as a woman of the 21st century. Being a mummy and working is over-achieving enough: you don't need to be cooking for six-course dinner parties at the weekend as well just to prove yourself. You have nothing to prove. And nothing to feel guilty about. There is no failure if you are concentrating on doing the best you can at home and at work, even if you don't always get it spot on.

The weeks are busy and hectic, and weekends should be as much as possible about fun and relaxation with your little family (once you've done the shopping, the washing, paid the bills …). Don't go driving yourself bananas doing the things you think you *should* be doing. What you really should be doing are the things that make you and your family happy, and don't add friction to what is already a busy, demanding schedule.

And most importantly, when your other half says, 'It's your turn for a lie-in,' the response is *always*, 'Okay dear.' (That really is a rule.)

- Keep calm
- Trust your instinct
- Listen to the baby expert: YOU

Acknowledgements

Huge thanks to ROAR Global, Random House and the staff, but more importantly the patients of Abbey Medical Centre.

And to my beloved Mr C who loves and supports me, but never, ever expects dinner on the table.

Index

Keep Calm: The New Mum's Manual

and 182
constipation 106, 107, 122,
124–8
craziness of life in the first
few weeks 79–83
crying 59–76
colic and 72–6
could my baby be ill?
65–6
crying in public 64–5
learning your baby's cries
60–2
leaving-to-cry method 30,
31
mother 79, 88–9, 138–9
reflux and 57
there isn't always an
answer 62–4
vaccinations and 189, 190
weaning and 211
what should I use to
soothe her? 66–71

development, baby 133–51
blame game 139–43
comparing notes 134–9
developmental stages and
ages that are important
143–50
1. big movement skills
145
2. little movement skills
147–8
3. baby talk 148–9
4. social skills 149–50

what to do if you are
worried 150–1
diarrhoea 122, 123, 128–9,
155, 161

expert, you are the 2–4
expressing 47, 49–50, 199

feeding 35–58
are there rules on
formula? 47–9
but you're a doctor, surely
you believe breast is
best? 40–3
feeding is not just about
the fluids 163–4
fussy eaters 206–7
how do I know my baby is
getting enough milk?
50–2
it's all gone tits up and I
want to stop 46–7
it's all gone tits up but I
want to carry on 43–5
reflux 57–8
should I be expressing?
49–50
weighing your baby 52–4
wind 54–7
you don't need to apolo-
gise 38–40
see also breastfeeding
formula:
are there rules on? 47–9
breast milk versus 41, 42,
43, 44, 46, 47–9

236

Keep Calm
The New
Mum's
Manual